KENT
DOG FRIENDLY
PUB WALKS

DAVID & HILARY STAINES

COUNTRYSIDE BOOKS
NEWBURY BERKSHIRE

First published 2019
Reprinted 2020
© 2019 David & Hilary Staines

COUNTRYSIDE BOOKS
3 Catherine Road
Newbury, Berkshire

To view our complete range of books please visit us at
www.countrysidebooks.co.uk

ISBN 978 1 84674 381 8

Photographs by David Staines

All materials used in the manufacture of this book carry FSC certification

Produced by The Letterworks Ltd., Reading
Designed and Typeset by KT Designs, St Helens
Printed by Holywell Press, Oxford

Contents

Walk

INTRODUCTION

This book is so much more than just about walking your dog and stopping off at the pub (or two). It's also about making the most of everything on the way, from things to see and explore to stunning landscapes packed with history and heritage – everything for a great time out in the great outdoors.

Kent and beer have gone hand in hand for hundreds of years. Enduring images of the county are hop gardens and oast houses so it's not surprising that Kent has an excellent selection of pubs. What better way to enjoy them, along with the outstanding variety of walks and scenery that the county provides, than with your dog?

We have chosen 20 dog friendly walks, centred on a wide variety of pubs that take in the best that the 'Garden of England' has to offer. There are plenty of walks in the countryside, but we also aim to be a little different and take you along clifftops, beaches, seafronts, through historic villages, alongside wide open marshes and past coastal towns. There really is so much to see and do.

Each of these walks has been specially surveyed for this book, focussing on dog friendliness.

Even where we were familiar with the routes, we have walked them again to ensure all the information is as up to date as possible. Unfortunately, we cannot rule out the fact that changes to paths, gates and stiles are not infrequent. If you find your route blocked by newly imposed obstructions, do not risk harming your animal by forcing them through or over them. If in any doubt about either the progress or safety of the route, or where a path has become unclear, obstructed, or for some reason non-existent, always be prepared to turn round and retrace your steps to the start. Don't risk harm to yourself or getting seriously lost. Use common sense in relation to your safety and the safety of your dog.

It's also wise to check at the bar that there is no problem leaving your car in the pub car park before or after your visit.

Enjoy!

David & Hilary Staines

PUBLISHER'S NOTE

We hope that you and your dog obtain considerable enjoyment from this book; great care has been taken in its preparation. In order to assist in navigation to the start point of the walk, we have included the nearest postcode, however, a postcode cannot always deliver you to a precise starting point, especially in rural areas. Although at the time of publication all routes followed public rights of way or permitted paths, diversion orders can be made and permissions withdrawn.

We cannot, of course, be held responsible for such diversion orders or any inaccuracies in the text which result from these or any other changes to the routes, nor any damage which might result from walkers trespassing on private property. We are anxious, though, that all the details covering the walks are kept up to date, and would therefore welcome information from readers which would be relevant to future editions.

The simple sketch maps that accompany the walks in this book are based on notes made by the author whilst surveying the routes on the ground. They are designed to show you how to reach the start and to point out the main features of the overall circuit, and they contain a progression of numbers that relate to the paragraphs of the text.

However, for the benefit of a proper map, we do recommend that you purchase the relevant Ordnance Survey sheet covering your walk – details of the relevant sheet are with each walk.

ADVICE FOR DOG WALKERS

The Countryside Code lists six steps to ensure your walk in the countryside is as safe as possible. These are:

- Keep your dog on a lead, or in sight at all times, be aware of what it's doing and be confident it will return to you promptly on command.

- Ensure it does not stray off the path or area where you have a right of access.

- When using access rights over open countryside and common land you must keep your dog on a short lead between 1 March and 31 July, to help protect ground nesting birds, and all year round near farm animals.

- Keep your dog on a lead around farm animals, particularly sheep, lambs and horses. This is for your own safety and for the welfare of the animals. A farmer may shoot a dog which is attacking or chasing farm animals without being liable to compensate the dog's owner.

- However, if cattle or horses chase you and your dog, it is safer to let your dog off the lead – don't risk getting hurt by trying to protect it. Your dog will be much safer if you let it run away from a farm animal in these circumstances and so will you.

- Everyone knows how unpleasant dog mess is and it can cause infections, so always clean up after your dog and get rid of the mess responsibly – 'bag it and bin it'. Make sure your dog is wormed regularly to protect it, other animals and people.

1 BOTANY BAY
4 miles (6.4 km)

This is a great seaside stroll incorporating clifftop, promenade and beach walks. We have chosen this route as it includes one of the few beaches in Kent which allows unrestricted dog access no matter what time of year. You will enjoy some fine sea views from the top of the cliffs and an opportunity to visit the chalk stacks at Botany Bay, one of the landmark features of the county.

How to get there: From the West take the A28 into central Margate. Where the road drops down onto the seafront take the left-hand B2051 turn signposted for Cliftonville. Continue along the B2051 as it winds along the clifftop. It will then turn sharp right inland. Keep following it for just over a mile inland. Continue along as it turns left then on the right-hand side immediately after the Nineteenth Hole pub, take the second left down Kingsgate Avenue. The Botany Bay Hotel is at the far end.
Sat Nav CT10 3LG.
Parking: There is free parking outside the Botany Bay Hotel (where the walk begins) and it has its own car park. There is also parking available in a small free car park at the end of Botany Road as well as unrestricted on-street parking in Percy Avenue.
OS Map: Explorer 150 Canterbury & Isle of Thanet.
Grid ref: TR392710.

Terrain: No road walking. Broad clifftop paths, promenades and sandy beaches. Apart from the way down to the beach and the slight short incline on the way up again, the walk is flat and easy.
Livestock: None.
Stiles: None.
Nearest vets: Briar House Veterinary Surgery, 13-15 Saint Peter's Road, Broadstairs, Kent CT10 2AG. ☎ 01843 863395.

THE PUB

BOTANY BAY HOTEL has a deservedly very popular dog friendly and modern bar, situated on the clifftop. There is plenty of seating in the bar area accommodating dogs and water bowls are provided. There is also outdoor seating on the deck overlooking the clifftop with relaxing ocean views. You can even stay at the hotel with your dog should you wish.
🌐 botanybayhotel.co.uk ☎ 01843 868 641

The Walk

❶ Turn left outside the pub following the path down towards the clifftop. If you would like to take a look at the chalk stacks, you have the chance to walk down the path on your immediate right which drops down to the beach. At the bottom turn right and the famous stacks will be facing you. However this beach (Botany Bay beach) is restricted with dogs not permitted after 10am between May and September. *It is said that Botany Bay found its name when smugglers were arrested here with contraband and on conviction were deported to Botany Bay in Australia. The stacks were formed when the sea eroded a crack in the headland and formed caves; further erosion formed an arch which later collapsed leaving*

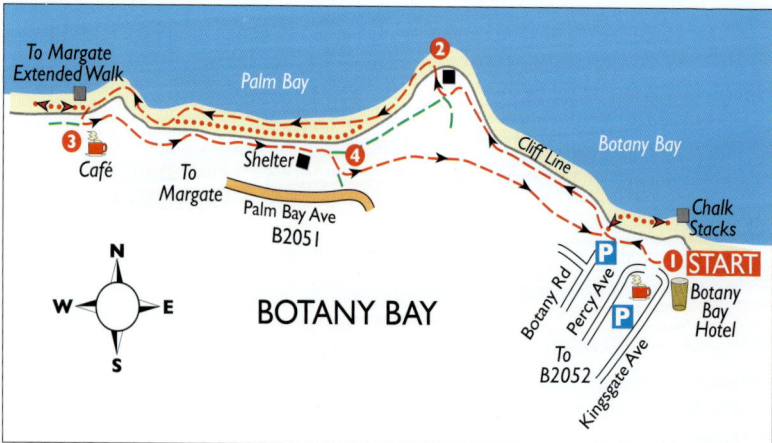

the stacks separated from the headland. To continue the walk, keep along the right-hand clifftop path until you get to the concrete water works building on the top of the headland.

2 Immediately after passing it, take the right-hand path which drops fairly steeply through the cliffs and down towards the beach. At the bottom turn left. At this point you need to be aware of the tides. You can easily check the tides by using the BBC weather website following the links and entering 102a Broadstairs as the required location. At high tide keep to the promenade but at lower tides after a while you will have the chance to drop down onto the sandy beach at Palm Bay. There are no restrictions on dog access to the sands here. You should be aware that exceptionally high tides may make even the promenade walk hazardous and in case of any doubt you should return to the cliff top. Walking either along the beach or the promenade follow the bay to the far end and round the headland. On your right-hand side you will see an open air sea water swimming pool. Now turn left and go up the gentle slope back to the clifftop.

3 Turn left at the top of the slope facing the Coastguard Station. Continue back along the broad clifftop path. On the right-hand side there will be the

Palm Bay Café if you need a refreshment stop. Continue along the path until you pass the large square shelter on the right-hand side. Shortly after the shelter, bear right along the wide tarmac path.

4 Before this path reaches the road bear left along the path with the hedge and house-line on your right-hand side. You now follow this all the way back to the start.

2 COLDRUM
2½ miles (4 km)

This is a walk with some real history – about 6,000 years of it. You start in the traditional village of Trottiscliffe and walk through typical Kentish landscape close to the side of the North Downs. There is a photogenic cluster of the Manor House, church and a few cottages on the way to the Coldrum Stones, a burial chamber dating from the Neolithic Period nearly 4,000 years BC. It's a little-known place; tourists may flock by the coachload to world famous Stonehenge, but at Coldrum there is no road so you have to walk, and the stones were put here 1,000 years earlier than those on Salisbury Plain!

How to get there: From the M26 Junction 2a initially follow the signs for Borough Green but at the traffic lights go ahead not right and then be immediately ready to take the second left a very short distance later. If you've come to a roundabout you've missed it! Follow this lane into Trottiscliffe, The George is on the left in the village centre.
Sat Nav ME19 5DR.
Parking: Either at The George or park considerately in the village.
OS Map: Explorer 148 Maidstone & the Medway Towns.
Grid ref: TQ640599.

THE PUB

THE GEORGE has been in the same family since 1945. It is tile-hung, Grade II listed and is thought to have been a medieval hall house dating from the 16th century. It faces the village green and features a variety of beamed rooms and bars. Dogs are welcome in all the bar areas. The White House across the road was once home to the famous artist Graham Sutherland who, in 1954 was given a 1,000 guinea commission to paint an official portrait of Sir Winston Churchill. Presented to Churchill on his 80th birthday, he hated it. It wasn't very flattering and was later burnt by order of his wife, Clementine.

🌐 thegeorgekent.co.uk ☎ 01732 822462

Terrain: A little bit of road walking, a very short distance initially through the village, but there is a pavement most of the way. Otherwise along paths and tracks, the only gradient is the climb up and around the stones themselves on the viewing path. One word of caution – after rainfall the path through Ryarsh Wood is very muddy. If you've not got a pair of wellies and have a hound that you mind getting dirty, wait until a dry spell for this walk!
Livestock: None encountered.
Stiles: Only to enter and exit the viewing path around the stones and they are dog friendly.
Nearest vets: Abbotsley Veterinary Group, 107 High St, West Malling, ME19 6NA. ☎ 01732 843080.

The Walk

❶ With your back to the pub turn left up Taylors Lane, there is a pavement on the left-hand side. You will pass some oast houses on the right and a farm on the left, both now restored to attractive residences. After the

crossroads take Green Lane on the right, signposted as a private road but this is the right of way for those on foot. At the end the footpath is on the right-hand side of the last house facing you. Take this path going straight ahead to the church facing you.

❷ Pass the 12th-century church of St Peter and St Paul on your left-hand side, and take the footpath on the left immediately after the last cottage. The path will climb up into the field and you will have a good view of the church and cottages behind you. At the end of the field, go through the gap in the fence and walk along the drive that is facing you. This soon becomes a track and then a path and after going through some trees it will emerge up into a field. Keeping the hedge-line on the right, at the end of the field turn right, along the track at the bottom.

3 A few metres later you will arrive at the Coldrum Stones. *The most prominent feature as you look up is the remains of the burial chamber, dating from around 3900 BC. A long barrow like this is not a graveyard, bodies were laid to rest elsewhere, and the bones were placed here some time later in a communal tomb. Behind the chamber was a mound of earth surrounded by sarsen stones. During the medieval period, places like Coldrum were considered pagan and many of the stones were deliberately removed or toppled and then buried. Archeologists excavating the site found two separate deposits of bones, each buried on top of a stone slab, one above the other.* There is a viewing path, with dog friendly stiles, that climbs up, circles the stones and drops down the other side. It's a great place to stop and soak up the atmosphere.

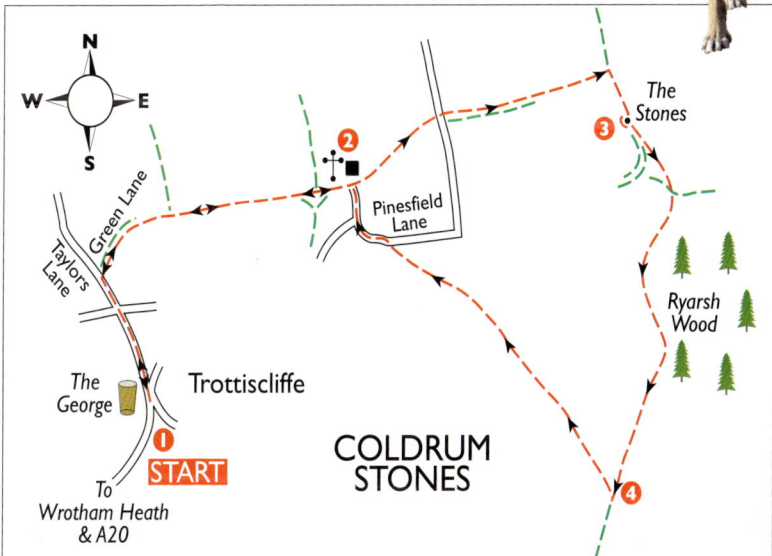

When you have finished your visit, continue along the tarmac track in the same direction. The tarmac will shortly veer to the right, but you need to take the footpath heading straight ahead. A few metres later the Ordnance Survey map shows this path as heading straight ahead, but on the ground it's actually a quick left and then right following the waymarkers up to the gate which you go through bringing you out on the path with a field on the left-hand side. You now follow this bridleway as it heads broadly in the same direction through Ryarsh Wood. *It is thought that several large sarsens south of the Coldrums might represent the remnants of another tomb, long since destroyed. You might spot a surprisingly large stone lying mostly buried along the path here.* Eventually you will come to a gate after which the path emerges into a field with the hedge-line on the left. Follow this path to the end of the field.

4 At the end of the field there is another gate. Don't go through it. (If you've come out onto a road you've gone too far and missed the turn.) You now need to do a 165° dog-leg right and take the path that has crossed the field from behind your right-hand shoulder. On our last visit it was not very clear and the route kept clear of crops was to the right-hand side of the actual right of way. If you look over into the following field the path is clear there, so just head for that. Failing that you can see the church tower in the distance. The right of way is in that direction, slightly to the right of the church tower. At the end of the first field, go through the gate following the waymarker in the same direction. Keep ahead across the fields in the same direction. At the far end bear left into the lane and follow it back to the church at point 2, and then retrace your steps back to the pub.

3 CONYER
2, 5 or 7 miles (3.2, 8 or 11.2 km)

This is a walk with a maritime theme. You start at Conyer Quay, at the end of one of the tidal inlets off the Swale Channel, the broad waterway which separates the north coast of Kent from the Isle of Sheppey. You pass the bustling boatyard and walk alongside the creek until you emerge at the creek's mouth which opens onto the broad Swale Channel. You can walk alongside this for as long and as far as you wish before returning at a lower level alongside the marshes. On returning to Conyer itself you can extend the walk by a further couple of miles, or if you don't want a long walk, just do the second half.

How to get there: Conyer is on the North Kent Marshes about a mile north of Teynham. Take the A2 out of Sittingbourne. At Teynham turn left into Station Road and once you are facing the level crossing turn right along The Crescent then first left into Conyer Road. You now just follow the road as it twists and turns through the fields to Conyer itself.
Sat Nav ME9 9HR.
Parking: There is on-street parking in the village outside The Ship Inn, on The Quay and Conyer Road.
OS Map: Explorer 149 Sittingbourne & Faversham.
Grid ref: TQ962645.

THE PUB

THE SHIP INN is right next to the creek. The original pub building was a baker's shop built in 1642 with a blacksmiths alongside. In 1802 it became an alehouse and part of the building then became known as The Ship Inn. It is now owned by Swale Marina, the main local boatyard. Recently refurbished, it features stripped wooden floors and exposed brickwork. There is a real fire, comfy armchairs, and a choice of cask ales, usually including

one from a small Kentish independent brewery. Old Dairy Red Top was our brew of choice on our last visit. There is a pleasant outside seating area at the front. Take a look at the 'brigg' by the front door. There is a traditional menu using locally sourced produce. Dogs are welcome but need to be on a lead.
⊕ shipinnconyer.co.uk
☎ 01795 520881

Terrain: A very short distance of road walking initially, then along well maintained broad paths. Apart from the height of the sea wall there are no gradients whatsoever.
Livestock: None.
Stiles: None.
Nearest vets: Swaleside Veterinary Surgery, 82 London Rd, Teynham, Sittingbourne ME9 9QH. ☎ 01795 520972.

The Walk

1 Turn right out of the pub. At the end of the road where the roadside 'the moorings' is facing you, turn right down the entrance road to Swale Marina. Do not take the footpaths on the left.

2 A few metres further along take the broad path on the left following the national cycle way signs. You now follow this path round the back of the marina bearing right when you can in order to keep the water constantly on your right-hand side. You will soon have fine views of Conyer Creek and its variety of boats and buildings across the water to your right-hand side. *As you walk you can see how remote and suitable for smuggling the area would have been in the past. In the 19th century Conyer also became known for its barge building. The last of the many sailing barges was built at the Conyer yard in 1914. Ship maintenance and repair is still a thriving activity in the creek.*

All you do now is keep following the path as it runs alongside the creek eventually emerging out onto the Swale where you will be able to enjoy fine views across the water on your right-hand side. You can turn back at any stage

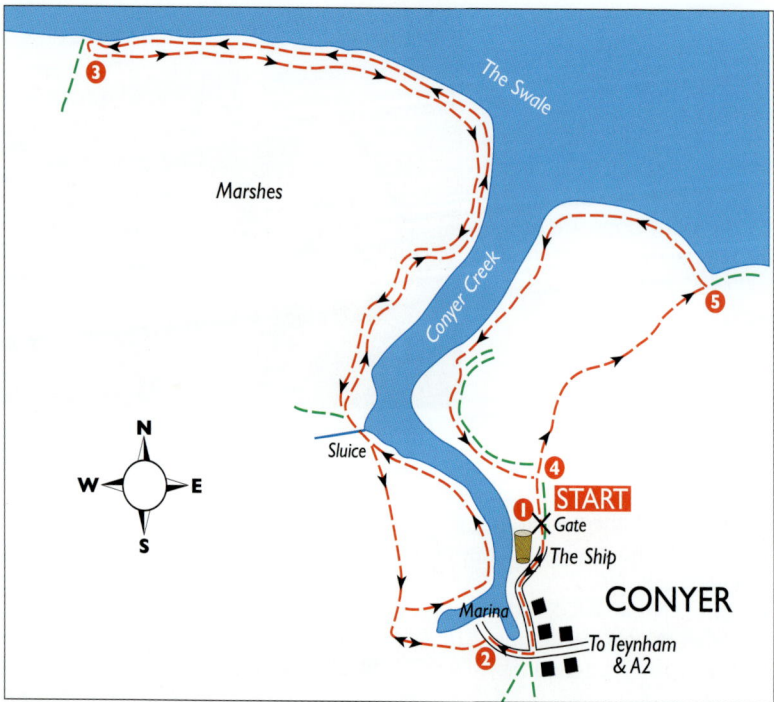

returning via the lower parallel path where you can take in the atmosphere of the marshes. We chose to continue ahead as far as the first bridge which crosses the water on the inland side.

3 If you have an Ordnance Survey map you may be tempted to return back along the track that now crosses the field. However, this should not be attempted as it is not a public right of way and although there is a footpath returning you to Conyer at the other side of Blacketts Farm, this would involve crossing the working livestock farmyard which would be unwise with a dog. When you have retraced your outward route as far as the sluice gate, if you wish you can take the footpath on the right-hand side which will give you a slight shortcut on the return to point 1. When you are back at The Ship Inn, to continue with the walk, carry on past the pub and go through the gate.

4 A short while later keep ahead along the narrower of the two paths where the wider tarmac track veers left. Continue along this path where the high hedges on both sides give way to open views across the fields towards the Swale.

5 When you reach the water take the footpath (ZR 686) on the left, keeping the Swale on your right-hand side. Keep on the higher level, not the lower

track. You now follow this along the waterside, bearing left alongside the bank of Conyer Creek where at low tide you can see the skeletal remains of a couple of barges. After a while the path dips away from the creek, then almost immediately bear right onto the tarmac track. This is an old brickworks road. *Conyer, which had seven brickfields, was famous for the role it played in supplying bricks to London in the 19th century. The clay and chalk here produced a yellow stock brick which was used across the capital for countless buildings, notably the long viaduct running from London Bridge to Greenwich which carried London's first ever railway line.* You now follow this tarmac track to point 4 and then retrace your steps a short distance back to the pub.

4 COOLING
3 miles (4.8 km)

This walk takes you through one of the lesser known parts of the Kent countryside, yet it is an area packed with historical interest. The churchyard is famous for being the inspiration for the opening chapter of one of Charles Dickens' most famous novels, *Great Expectations*.

How to get there: From the M2, exit at J1, on to the A289 for Grain. Exit the A289 at the second junction, signed for the B2000, Wainscott and Cliffe. Turn left on to the B2000. After you have passed through the village of Cliffe Woods take the minor road (Cooling Road) on the right signposted for Cooling. Follow this as it twists and turns passing the church on the right until you come to the pub on the right-hand side at the end of the village.
Sat Nav ME3 8DP.
Parking: Either at or outside The Horseshoe & Castle pub.
OS Map: Explorer 148 Maidstone & the Medway Towns.
Grid ref: TQ759760.

Terrain: Flat and easy with some road walking along quiet lanes and byways.
Livestock: None encountered.
Stiles: None.
Nearest vets: Stanhope Veterinary Centre, 29 Stanhope Rd, Rochester ME2 3EJ. ☎ 01634 713065.

THE PUB

THE HORSESHOE & CASTLE is a traditional country inn with a variety of seating areas inside including comfy sofas and a terrace at the front overlooking the lane. The beer quality is good and as well as meals and homemade cakes there are dog treats on sale at the bar.
🌐 horseshoeandcastle.com ☎ 01634 221691

A short diversion halfway through the walk will take you to the **SIX BELLS** in Cliffe at 181 Church Street. There is an unpretentious and traditional feel to this Shepherd Neame house, with wooden floors and exposed brick walls. Outside there is a patio and a large beer garden. A range of homemade bar snacks and traditional pub meals are available seven days a week. Just behind the pub is the church with views across the marshes to the Thames Estuary.
🌐 sixbellscliffe.co.uk ☎ 01634 221459

The Walk

1 With your back to The Horseshoe & Castle turn left down the lane. A few metres later take the footpath on the left. As soon as it emerges into the field turn sharp right following the backs of the house and St James' church on the right-hand side. *The churchyard at St James was the inspiration for the opening chapter of the book* Great Expectations, *in which the hero of the story,*

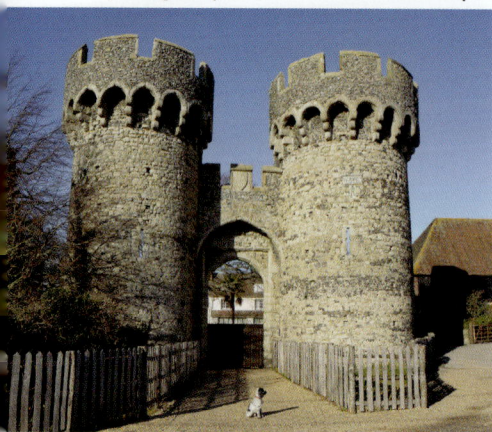

Pip, meets convict, Magwitch who has escaped from a prison hulk moored in the nearby Thames Estuary. Today you can stand in the churchyard complete with the row of children's tombstones noted by Dickens in the novel (now inevitably referred to as Pip's graves) but it will be container ships you can see as you look down towards the estuary, not the prison hulks of Dickens' time. Keep ahead at the lane. You can walk on the field on the left-hand side to avoid walking in the road. You will soon pass Cooling Castle on the right-hand side. *The castle was built in the 1380s to guard against French raids into the Thames Estuary. It was originally on the riverbank but land reclamation has seen the shore recede. In 1554 after only eight hours of siege it was badly damaged during a rebellion by Kentish landowner Sir Thomas Wyatt against Queen Mary and was subsequently abandoned. The 600-year-old gatehouse is right next to the lane but the rest is strictly private property.* Continue ahead a few metres.

2 Where the lane crosses the stream take the footpath on the right. Continue across the field, through the gate and later over a bridge across a stream. When you come to the next gate bear right following the waymarker to the right-hand side of the tree line. When you emerge onto the lane turn right then a short distance later when you have come to Rye Street Farm take the footpath on the left. Walk straight across this field. *On your right-hand side are views of the London Gateway at Thames Haven.* Initially the path will be indistinct. You are heading towards a gap in the houses which are on the horizon. The gap will be slightly to the right of the electricity wires where they meet the houses. Go through the gap in the houses and turn immediately left along the residential road.

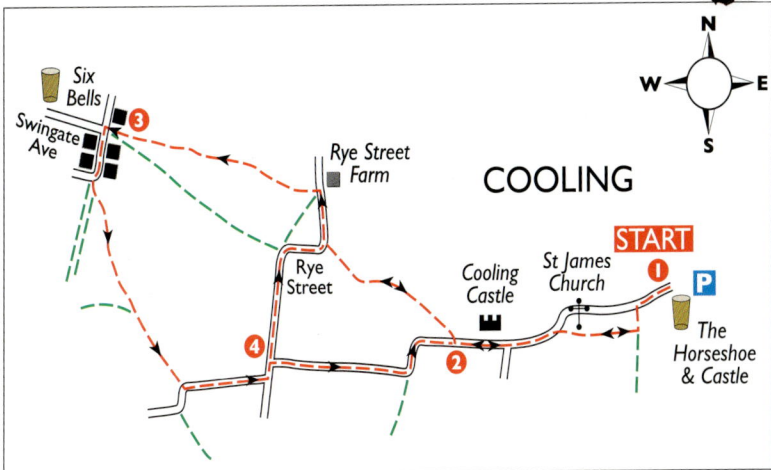

3 If you wish to visit the Six Bells in Cliffe, don't turn left but go straight ahead along Swingate Avenue facing you. Where it emerges onto Church Street the pub will be to your right. Continuing on the walk, having turned left continue to the end. The footpath is at the end to the right-hand side of the final houses. Follow the footpath sign, but as soon as you are in the field do not take the track straight ahead, instead bear left at the waymarker taking the path diagonally across the field at an approximate 30° angle from the track. Follow this path to the far end of the field. Where it emerges onto the lane turn left. Then take the next left. A few metres later you have a choice.

4 You can either turn right here and follow the quiet road back to the start or keep ahead and after the lane turns to the right regain the footpath back to the starting point.

5 CROCKHAM HILL

2 miles (3.2 km)

This is a fairly short walk through the meadows and fields in the shadow of the North Downs. The area has been home to many influential people. Famous figures such as Churchill and Gladstone had houses close by whilst the social reformer and National Trust co-founder Octavia Hill lived in the village and chose to be buried in the churchyard rather than Westminster Abbey.

How to get there: Take the A25 through Westerham. After you have passed through the town take the left turn at Goodley Stock Road passing Squerryes Court on the left-hand side. At the far end turn left onto the B269. This road will drop down into the village. The pub is on the right.

Sat Nav TN8 6RB.

Parking: There is on-street parking in the village or at the pub.

OS Map: Explorer 147 Sevenoaks & Tonbridge. **Grid ref:** TQ442505.

Terrain: A few metres of road walking, a very short distance initially in the village. Thereafter footpaths, mostly across fields. Easy gradients.
Livestock: Sheep can be encountered at various places.
Stiles: A few, but all dog friendly.
Nearest vets: Nelson Mark, The Old Cornstore, London Rd, Westerham TN16 1DR. ☎ 01959 569472.

THE PUB

THE ROYAL OAK has been a beer and cider house since the 19th century, however, parts of the building are thought to be at least 500 years old. There used to be a 35-foot well in the bar which the pub notes was recorded in the 1960s as a possible safe supply of drinking water in the event of an atomic war. Less potentially hazardous are the beers showcased today. The award-winning pub is the second tied house of the local Westerham brewery which has revived many of the much-loved flavours of the old Black Eagle Brewery, which closed in 1965. There are comfy leather sofas on a stripped wood floor, with original cartoons and old local photographs on the walls, and a log fire in the right-hand bar where dogs are welcome. There is also a small garden behind the car park.
🌐 royaloakcrockhamhill.co.uk ☎ 01732 866335

The Walk

● ●

1 With the pub behind you, turn left and walk up the hill. Where the roads diverge at the village sign, bear left up the hill. A few metres later turn left into Oakdale Lane and follow it to the end. At the large house at the end take the footpath on the left. At the bottom of the next field cross the stile and bear right through the trees. Where the path emerges into a field, cross the stile and follow the waymarker keeping the hedge-line on your right-hand side. At the other end of the field cross the next stile and keep going in the same direction. You will see a large ornamental lake on your right-hand side.

2 As soon as you are no longer level with the lake, at the large tree you need to turn sharp 90° left. You will now be following the

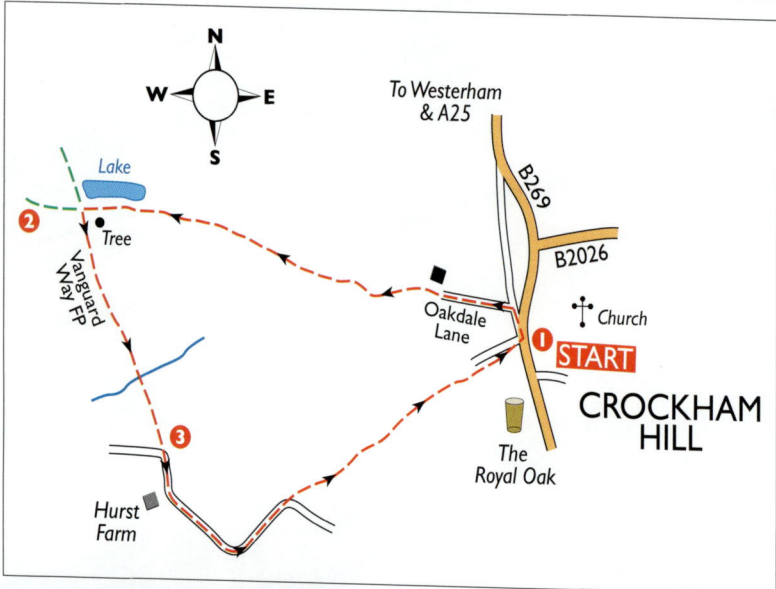

Vanguard Way long-distance footpath. The path here can be indistinct but if you stand with your back to the large isolated tree and look for the oast house of Hurst Farm, you will see the correct direction across the field. At the other side of the field there is a double stile through the hedge-line. The footpath crosses the Kent Brook on a small footbridge. On the other side keep following the footpath ahead with the fence-line on your right-hand side, then turn right through the gate and out onto the lane.

3 Follow the lane through two left-hand bends then take the bridleway ahead of you once the lane has curved to the right. Follow the bridleway up the hill and at the top, when it emerges onto a residential road, keep going straight ahead to the far end. At the end turn right and you will be almost next to the pub.

6 FARNBOROUGH
2 miles (3.2 km)

This is a simple walk through fields that are very popular with dog walkers. Farnborough is only 15 miles from Charing Cross and lies on the very edge of the Greater London built up area. Whilst many places in suburbia claim to be a 'village', Farnborough is still a real village where you can walk straight into open fields. It is where London ends and Kent begins, and it is into these fields that our walk takes us.

How to get there: From the M25 Junction 4 follow the signs for Bromley. After you have left the main motorway (not the connecting spur), at the 4th roundabout turn left. Cross the next mini roundabout and at the top of the hill you will be in Farnborough village. The pub is on the right-hand side.
Sat Nav BR6 7BA.
Parking: There is unrestricted on-street parking close to the pub. There is an alternative car park at the Green Roof Café.
OS Map: Explorer 147 Sevenoaks & Tonbridge. **Grid ref:** TQ442643.

Terrain: Initially a short distance along a pavement but then along well defined footpaths through fields. The walk drops downhill and then back up again but the gradients are easy and not too strenuous.
Livestock: None.
Stiles: None.
Nearest vets: All Creatures Clinic, 51 Windsor Drive, Chelsfield, Kent, BR6 6EY. ☎ 01689 856220.

THE PUB

CHANGE OF HORSES is a 400-year-old traditional community pub. Its name originates from the practice of stage coaches stopping to change their horses at the stables which were once part of the premises, although in reality it only changed its name from The New Inn in 1973. There are outside seats at the front and a garden at the rear. Water bowls and dog treats are available.

⊕ changeofhorses.co.uk ☎ 01689 852949

Alternatively we can recommend the **GREEN ROOF CAFÉ** further along the walk. It bills itself as both eco-friendly and the most picturesque café in the locality. Whilst dogs are not permitted inside, it is very popular with dog walkers with plenty of outdoor tables, some on a deck overlooking a pond and walled garden with other tables under a deep canopy. The quality of the breakfasts outshines many other more pretentious establishments! Open from 9.30am weekends, 10am weekdays.

⊕ thegreenroofcafe.co.uk ☎ 01689 855439

The Walk

1 With your back to the Change of Horses turn left along Farnborough High Street. *This part of the road was once the main stage coach route between London and the south coast, becoming a turnpike in 1749. This history is reflected in the village sign.* In the centre of the village, just before the bench and village sign, turn right down Church Road. With your dog on a lead, follow the path through the lychgate into the churchyard as the road drops down on the left. *In 1833 the level of the road was lowered to make passage easier for the horse-drawn coaches. This is why*

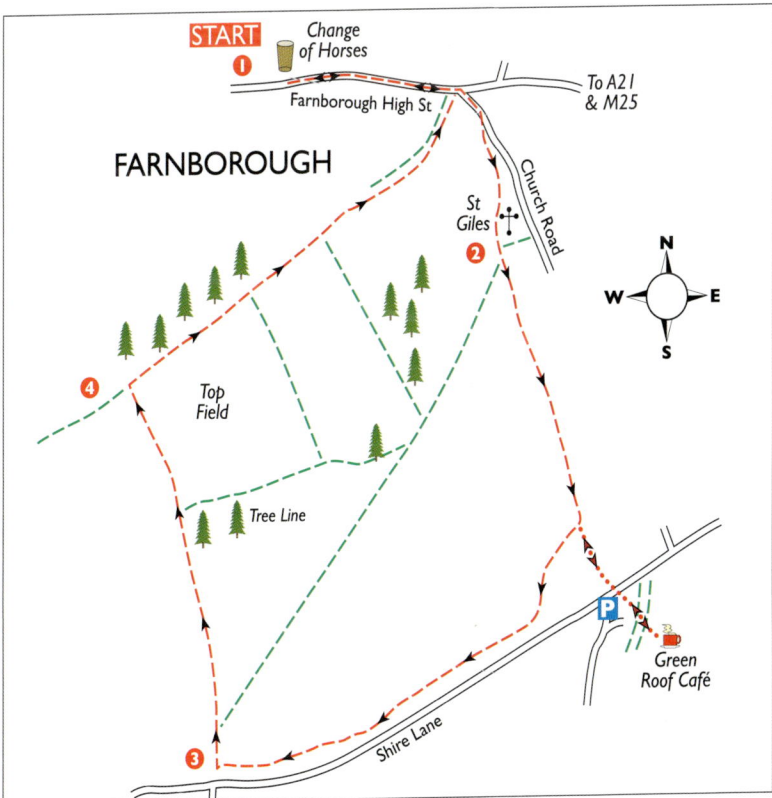

the road now sinks below the level of the ground to either side at this point. Follow the path as it passes the church and emerges into a large field. For about 1500 years, it is believed, a church has stood on this high piece of land to the south of the village. The building has been altered a great many times over the centuries. The Nave dates from the 12th century, whilst the small spire only dates from the 1950s. Church records from the 1700s show rewards were offered for badgers' heads and the carcasses of polecats and hedgehogs. Today, more animal friendly, you will sometimes find a dog's water bowl at the church door.

2 Go through the gate and follow the path downhill keeping the tree line on your left-hand side. At the bottom you have a choice. If you want to visit the Green Roof Café, keep ahead in the same direction through the trees. You will then cross a road, take care crossing as some cars take this lane at speed. Follow the path a few metres through the trees on the other side and then cross the car park in front of you. Take the path directly in front of you and then keep ahead a few metres up the tarmac track to the café.
If you don't want to visit the café bear right at the bottom of the field following the path along the field boundary.

3 When the path ends next to the road with North End Lane on the other side of the road, turn sharp right up the broad path heading up the field. Go through the tree line and keep going uphill through the Top Field. When you come to the woods on your right, turn right.

4 There will soon be some benches on your left where you can sit and admire the view from the top of the hill. To your far left on a clear day you can see the spire of Chelsfield church whilst ahead of you is the High Elms Country Park. Out of sight on your right is Biggin Hill Airport. Come here when one of the famous Biggin Hill air shows is on and you will get a free view, although the fields will be busy with plenty of local people doing the same thing! Continue along this top path and you will soon notice on your left a parallel trackway in the trees. Now take this trackway which will take you back to the village centre. Turn left at the end and follow your outward route.

7 FOLKESTONE
2 miles (3.2 km)

Anyone who knew **Folkestone of old** will be stunned by the change which has taken place in recent years, both to the area of the Lower Leas and around the harbour. This walk celebrates both the regeneration of Victorian heritage and also provides some fascinating contrasts. Although a town walk, it features clifftops, a country park, the beach and harbour; nearly all in a traffic-free environment. If at all possible try to do this walk at a time when the harbour arm is open. Check www.folkestoneharbourarm.co.uk.

How to get there: From the M20 Junction 13 (the end of the motorway) follow the signs for Folkestone harbour. At the bottom of the hill follow the harbour around and after the Burstin Hotel turn right into Marine Parade which you follow to the far end.
Sat Nav CT20 2DR.
Parking: In the public car park at the end of Marine Parade. Although this is only a relatively short walk, there are plenty of attractions along the way. If you choose to visit the pub and take some time at the harbour arm you will need to pay for at least four hours of parking.
OS Map: Explorer 138 Dover, Folkestone & Hythe.
Grid ref: TR227356.

KENT – Dog Friendly Pub Walks

THE PUB **THE HARBOUR INN** is another example of Folkestone's regeneration. Formerly the True Briton and with a long history associated with the sea it reopened in 2018 with an unsurprisingly nautical theme. It features stripped floors with wooden seats and benches and candlelit tables with bunches of hops hanging from the ceiling. Dogs are welcome in the area to the right-hand side of the bar.

🌐 theharbourinnfolkestone.co.uk ☎ 01303 487260

Terrain: Well laid out paths throughout although there is a steep climb up steps from sea level to the clifftop. The rest of the route is flat and easy. There is a short distance of road walking down the Road of Remembrance and around the harbour.
Livestock: None.
Stiles: None.
Nearest vets: Abbeywell Veterinary Clinic, 2-3 Majestic Parade, Sandgate Road, Folkestone, CT20 2BZ. ☎ 01303 227179.

The Walk

❶ At the end of the car park go through the barrier leading onto the wide path with lamp posts entering the Lower Leas Coastal Park. *In 1784 a huge landslip produced a new strip of land between the beach and cliff-line. In Victorian times it was developed into a pleasure garden but by the 1990s had fallen on hard times. Now, this delightful trail of paths has been returned to its former glory and leads you through swathes of beautiful trees and plants with occasional glimpses of the sea.* You can choose whether to follow the main footpath or branch off onto the smaller one on your left depending on what you would like to see. If you remain on the main path you will need to put your dog on a lead at the point where it passes through the children's play area. *Towards the end you will pass the Old Toll House on your left-hand side. Until 1973 the main path that you have walked along was a privately owned road giving access to Folkestone Harbour and payment for its use had to be made here.*

❷ When you come to a small car park turn right up the recently renovated Metropole Steps which climb up to the Upper Leas. At the top you will see two of Folkestone's historic hotels facing you. Turn right here and follow the wide

34

footpath along the Upper Leas with the sea on your right-hand side. As you walk along you will see various pieces of newly installed contemporary artwork. *The Upper Leas is Folkestone's unique clifftop promenade, it was the place where the well-to-do took the coastal air in the Victorian and Edwardian period. Note the bandstand on the left-hand side, built in an Art Nouveau style in 1895. You will also pass the Leas Cliff Hall (1927) and the Cliff Funicular Lift (1885).*

The lift operates using water and gravity and its builders, Waygood-Otis, went on to make the world's first commercial escalator. It emits no pollution and recycles all of the water used to drive the cars.

3 After a while you will pass beneath the Step Short Memorial Arch. *This commemorates the millions of men and women who passed through Folkestone in military service during the First World War. Each soldier would have gone down 'The Slope', as it was then known. At the top of the hill they would have heard the order 'Step Short', an instruction to shorten their stride in order to negotiate the gradient safely.* The road is now The Road of Remembrance which, keeping ahead,

you now walk down. Note the artwork on the opposite side of the road and the endless flow of knitted poppies on the railings. Take care here as the pavement is a little narrow. At the bottom of the hill keep going ahead taking care of the busy traffic coming round the corner. A few metres later, at the end of the next road, The Harbour Inn is on the right-hand side.

To continue the walk, cross the road and bear left towards the fountains. Keep the harbour on your right-hand side. At the other side of the fountains take the steps up onto the old railway viaduct. At the top turn right. You will have some great views as the viaduct crosses the Inner and Outer Harbour. This is the start of the most significant area of regeneration. At the end keep going ahead through the platforms of the old Folkestone Harbour Station. *Folkestone Harbour was part of the first ever regular international rail-sea-rail journey in the world when (beating rival Dover) the ferries started conveying London to Paris passengers in 1844. The last ferry sailed in 2001 and the harbour and its facilities became increasingly derelict. Key historical elements are now being restored including artwork such as Anthony Gormley's iron sculpture figure, one in a series of 100 placed worldwide, and the station was reopened for pedestrians in 2018.*

4 If the harbour arm is open go through the gates. The redundant port facilities here have been swept away and the historic granite pier restored. In summer, it is now littered with an eclectic mix of bars and eateries and is well worth spending a while here to soak up the vibrant atmosphere.

5 Return to point 4. Now take the boardwalk across the beach on the left just before the station canopies. With more art installations on the way, follow this across the shingle to the far end and the car park is on the right-hand side.

8 IGHTHAM

3½ miles (5.6 km)

Starting on **Shipbourne Common this walk** takes you through the Fairlawne Estate and, whilst taking in some great views on the way, brings you right past the National Trust's 14th-century moated manor house, Ightham Mote. Originally dating from around 1320 the house has been owned by medieval knights, courtiers to Henry VIII and high society Victorians. It is surrounded on all sides by a square moat, crossed by three bridges. Dogs should be on leads where the signage directs on the Fairlawne Estate.

How to get there: The pub is prominently on Stumble Hill in Shipbourne on the main A227 exactly half way between Borough Green and Tonbridge. You can't miss it!
Sat Nav TN11 9PE.
Parking: In the car park by the common, opposite the pub.
OS Map: Explorer 147 Sevenoaks & Tonbridge. **Grid ref:** TQ591521.

> **Terrain:** A mix of open countryside and woodland using footpaths, bridleways and country lanes which can be muddy in winter. A very short distance of road walking in two places along quiet roads.
> **Livestock:** Potential for livestock at various places.
> **Stiles:** There are wired stiles so this walk is not suitable for dogs that you cannot assist over. The greatest height is 2 feet from the highest step board over the top of the most awkward stile.
> **Nearest vets:** Sevenoaks Veterinary Surgery, 104 Seal Road, Sevenoaks, Kent, TN14 5AU. ☎ 01732 740999.

THE PUB

THE CHASER INN is a popular Grade II listed pub built in a colonial style in 1880. It sits next to the parish church looking out onto the common. Its name is associated with the nearby Fairlawne Estate where steeplechase horses, including the late Queen Mother's were trained. It's an interesting building with several rooms leading off the central bar area and an impressive barrel-vaulted dining room. Dogs are welcome in the front bar, courtyard room and garden where water bowls and dog treats are available. You'll need to book ahead for Sunday lunch.
⊕ thechaser.co.uk ☎ 01732 810360

The Walk

1 From the car park, set off along Common Road in the opposite direction to the pub. Pass the tennis courts on the left and at the village sign turn left at the small crossroads. Go down the side road, bear left after a few metres and turn right down the residential road with the converted oast house on the left. Continue ahead down the narrow path when the road veers to the right. Cross the open field and at the bottom cross the bridge over the stream and go over the stile. Keep ahead following the right-hand hedge line. At the next gate go ahead and follow the estate drive in the same direction passing an ornamental lake on your left. Just after you have passed the lake, where there is a junction of drives, bear right and go up through the trees across the grass and through the wooden gate at the top. Then bear left towards the crown of the hill where you will find a yellow marker pole guiding the way. *Ahead of you is Fairlawne House, built in the 17th century by Sir Henry Vane the Elder, Secretary of State to Charles I and later beheaded by Charles II.*

2 At the grassy crossroads of paths, keep in the same direction following

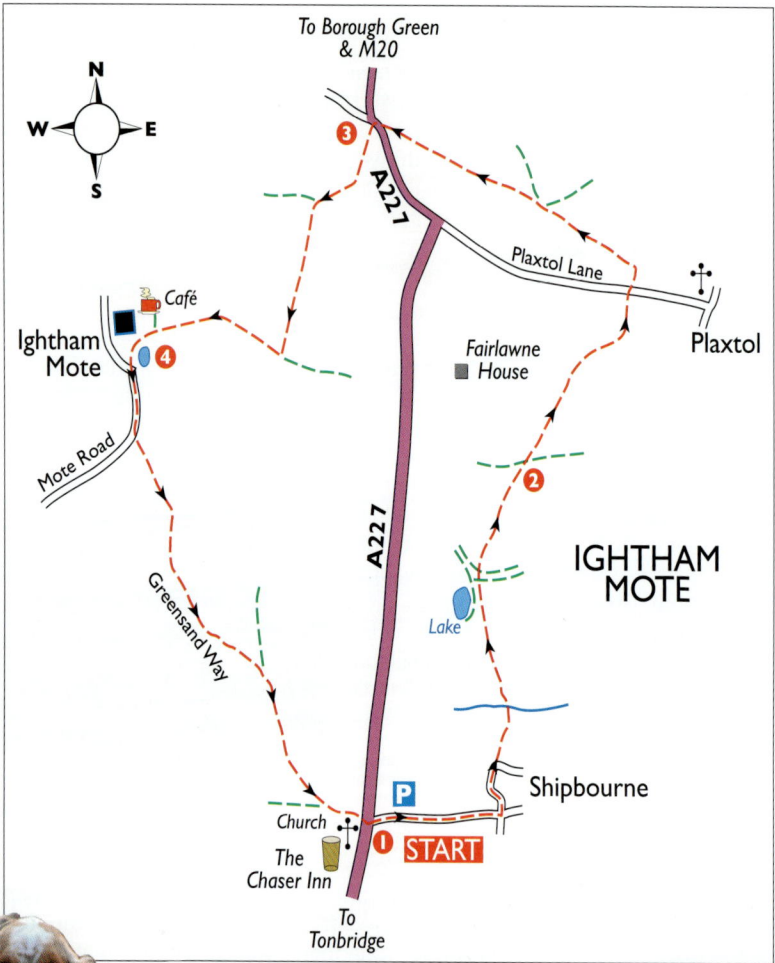

the posts, bearing right away from the house. Go over the stile in the next fence; keep following the path gently uphill with views of Plaxtol church in the distance. Skirt the wooden fence on the left. At the lane cross the stile. Having crossed the road keep going ahead a few metres then turn left following the footpath as it gently climbs uphill. The path will eventually take you through some woods. Put your dog on a lead and go through the gate at the end. Take care crossing the main road.

3 Having crossed the road take the sharp left-hand bridle path down through the woods. Continue to follow the path downhill and, passing a small clearing with a view back towards Shipbourne on the left, bear slightly right and continue on this path. Where a path turns off to the right, go into the woods and keep to the blue waymarked bridle path as it continues to drop downhill. Where it emerges into a field you get some great views ahead. Keep following the path down to the end of the field. Turn right at the junction at the bottom and follow the track. Where it emerges onto a tarmac drive you will be at Ightham Mote. For the café turn right through the car park.

4 To continue with the walk, keep ahead as the drive drops down with fine views of the house on the right-hand side. *Unlike most houses of its type, no buildings inside the moat were ever demolished so many still look as they would*

have done in the Middle Ages. As late as 1951 the house was saved at auction for £5,500 by three local men following a suggestion it could be demolished to recover the valuable lead from the roofs. It was later the home of a wealthy American who made urgent repairs before leaving it to the National Trust. Follow the drive left after the house and up towards the lane. You will need to walk along the lane for a few metres but then take the first footpath on the left. This is the Greensand Way long-distance footpath which you will now be following. Where it emerges from some woods and drops downhill bear left. Keep ahead over various stiles following the public footpath waymarkers. Continue along the path all the way back to the church. Towards the end it becomes a little indistinct where it crosses a maintained grassed area, but just keep going in the same direction. You need to cross the stile on the right-hand side as you approach the church. Having crossed the stile turn sharp left taking the path through the churchyard to the left of the church. When you are facing the main road the starting point will be ahead of you.

9 IVYCHURCH
2½ miles (4 km)

The village of Ivychurch sits right in the middle of Romney Marsh, which has for ever been associated with the smuggling trade. Smugglers known locally as 'Owlers' took advantage of this windswept landscape with its numerous hidden paths and lanes to hide and then move cargo on from the beaches for distribution inland. In this walk we follow in their footsteps using some of those same little-used routes across the Marsh.

How to get there: From the M20 Junction 10 follow the signs for the A2070 and Brenzett. Once the A2070 has dropped onto the Romney Marsh after Ham Street, follow the sign left for Ivychurch. The Bell pub is on the left-hand side as you enter the village.
Sat Nav TN29 0AN.
Parking: There is on-street parking in Ivychurch Road.
OS Map: Explorer 125, Romney Marsh, Rye & Winchelsea.
Grid ref: TR027276.

THE BELL INN is a proper community pub and has won many CAMRA awards. St George's church forms an impressive backdrop to the large and well cared for beer garden. Dogs are welcomed inside on the tiled area provided they don't get on the furniture!
🌐 thebellinnromneymarsh.co.uk ☎ 01797 344355

The Walk

. . . .

1 With your back to the pub turn left along the lane. Ignore the first footpath on the right, although it takes you in the right direction it becomes too indistinct to properly navigate.

2 Take the next byway on the right with the sign stating unsuitable for motor vehicles. Soon it narrows into a footpath with blackthorn hedges on both sides. *This is what many lanes*

would have looked like in the Owlers' time. Imagine the scene here 200 years ago with a moonlit mist rising off the deserted marshes as a gang of up to 200 men moved their illegal cargo through here from beach to storage in the isolated Marsh cottages and church. After a while the hedges will drop back and you will have open unfenced fields on both sides, criss-crossed by irrigation ditches. These are too numerous to put on the map. Listen out for the 'laughing frog',

it's a large species of frog which was accidentally introduced to Britain in 1935. Twelve Marsh Frogs were brought back from Hungary to a garden pond just off the Romney Marsh. They all quickly escaped and spread through the

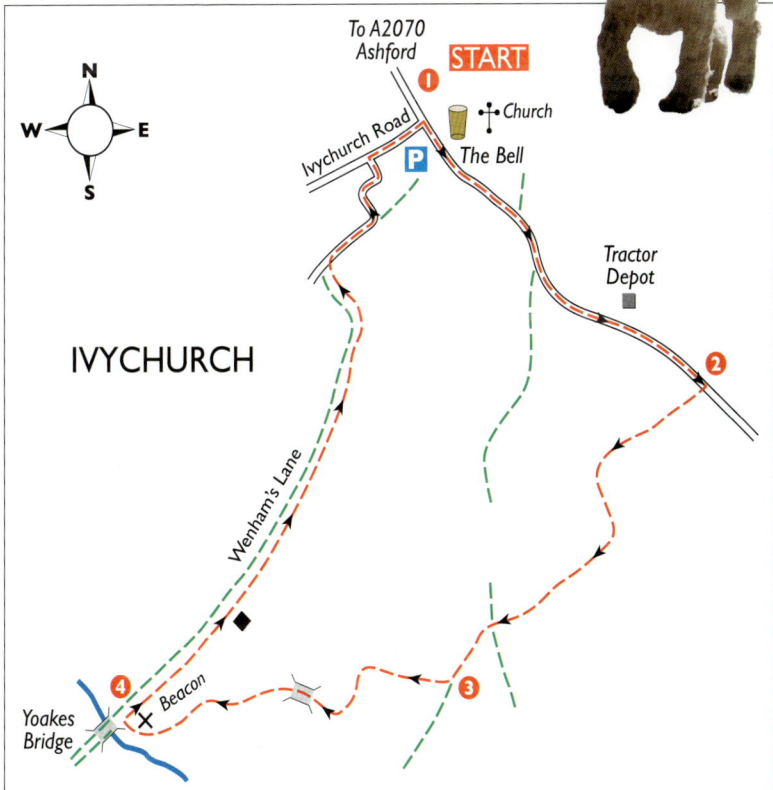

N
W   E
S

To A2070
Ashford

START

Ivychurch Road

P

Church

The Bell

Tractor
Depot

IVYCHURCH

Wenham's Lane

2

Beacon

4

Yoakes
Bridge

X

3

network of ditches on the Marsh. By 1937 they were so widespread that there were complaints to the Ministry of Health about the noise. Take note when a footpath (with bridges across the ditches on both sides of the path that you are on) crosses. Keep ahead but be prepared to take the next unsigned path on the right.

3 You now follow this path; initially it is a little indistinct. You can just see a small cottage ahead of you about ½ mile away in the distance. The path swings left and then right. Once it has swung right make sure you have a watercourse on both sides of the path which is on top of a slightly raised embankment. If you are walking along the side of a field with a drainage ditch only on your right side and with, a few metres later also on the right, a small brick bridge through a slightly raised embankment, then you've missed the right-hand swing. So you will need to retrace your steps. You should be walking on top of the slightly raised embankment and crossing over the bridge. Just follow the path as it follows the watercourses, in places it will be a little indistinct. In the near distance you will see a curiously shaped metal framework. It is a landing beacon for Lydd Airport and the path will skirt it to the left-hand side.

4 When the path emerges onto a lane with the beacon on the right, turn right along the lane. You now follow this quiet and empty lane all the way back to Ivychurch. No vehicles passed us for its entire length. As it nears the village it twists and turns a few times. When it finally emerges onto Ivychurch Road, turn right and you will soon be back at the start.

10 LEEDS
2½ miles (4 km)

This walk takes you through the parkland of Leeds Castle, one of the county's top tourist attractions which bills itself as the 'loveliest castle in the world'. It's an easy walk along footpaths through the estate and you get some great views of the castle. You should, however, keep strictly to the public footpath and not explore further as the castle charges for admission to the grounds and does not allow dogs. Castle staff are vigilant but on the public footpath you are fine as the signage confirms. Walk the route early in the day before the full grounds open to visitors and you'll feel like you've got the whole place to yourselves.

How to get there: From Junction 8 on the M20 follow the signs for Lenham but then turn right at the second roundabout. Follow the lane past the castle entrance and church, and the pub is in the village on the left-hand side.
Sat Nav ME17 1RN.
Parking: At The George Inn, or considerately on the adjacent side road. The car park at the church is private.
OS Map: Explorer 148 Maidstone & the Medway Towns.
Grid ref: TQ823531.

Terrain: A little road walking along quiet lanes. Gently undulating paths and tracks through the castle parkland.
Livestock: Sheep can be encountered at various places and waterfowl around the lakes.
Stiles: None.
Nearest vets: Harrietsham Vets, Unit 9, Roebuck Business Park, Ashford Rd, Harrietsham, Maidstone, ME17 1AB. ☎ 01622 858666.

THE GEORGE INN is Grade II listed; parts of it date back to 1652 although most of the building dates from the 19th century. Owned by Kentish brewer Shepherd Neame, it's a welcoming country pub with a real fire in winter. Dogs are welcome in the bar area and there is also a small patio at the front and a nice garden at the side.
⊕ georgeinnleeds.co.uk
☎ 01622 861314

The Walk

· ·

1 With the pub behind you, turn right up the lane taking the path next to the road. A short distance later, at the top of the hill, turn right into the church entrance following the public footpath signs and go through the churchyard gate.

2 Take the footpath to the right of the church and follow it through the churchyard. Go through the gate at the end and follow the path across the next field. Cross the lane through the gates and keep ahead. Don't bear right at the other side of the lane. Carry on ahead through the gate into the cricket ground keeping to the left-hand boundary and go through the gate at the end.

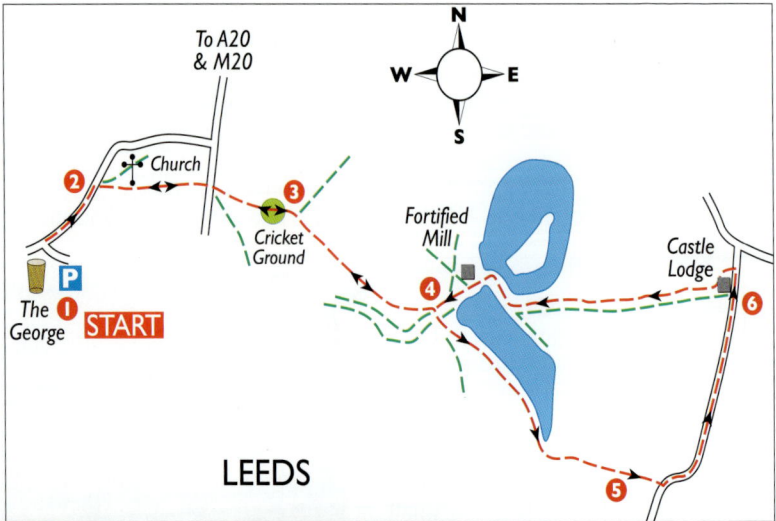

3 When you have exited the gate from the cricket ground you will be beneath a small clump of trees. Take the path ahead but bearing slightly right out of the trees. Keep a look out for sheep grazing here. Look down the hill towards the tarmac drive to the right of an isolated tree and you will see a yellow marker post indicating the right of way. In the summer the path will be shown as a mown course through the meadow. Where the tarmac drive enters the trees at the other end of the sloping meadow go through the gate noting the direction of the waymarker arrow on the post.

4 After you have passed a small service car park on the right, turn right off the tarmac drive immediately after the bushes. A yellow waymarker post points the way. Now go across the grass following the next waymarker post and down the slight gradient. At the fence-line at the bottom the right of way goes through the left-hand gate. With good views of the castle on your left, cross the tiny bridge over the brook and head up the path between the trees. *The first castle here was built by the Normans in 1119. In 1278 it was bought by the wife of Edward I and while remaining in royal hands until Tudor times it was the home of six medieval queens. Edward VI gave the castle to a courtier and it was later owned by some of the most influential families in the country. In 1926 it*

was bought by an Anglo-American heiress who left the castle to a charitable trust that is now responsible for its upkeep. Carry on in the same direction taking the path through the gate into the woods. Cross the stream and continue along the path until it emerges into a lane.

5 Turn left up the lane, following it uphill for a little while.

6 A few metres before the lane emerges onto a main road take the signposted footpath on the left. Drop down the steps and bear left at the bottom. Turn right along the tarmac drive and follow it to the very end. Yellow waymarker posts confirm this is the right way. With the castle very close by across the moat,

turn right at the end and when the castle entrance over a bridge across the moat is on your right, turn left. You will be at the remains of the 13th-century fortified mill and barbican. A concrete public footpath sign pointing the way at ground level confirms the route. Now follow this tarmac path very slightly uphill. Don't bear right. Another ground level concrete footpath sign confirms the way. You will shortly be back at point 4, where you can retrace your steps to the pub.

11 LENHAM & THE PILGRIMS' WAY

2½ miles (4 km)

This walk features a choice of two contrasting pubs at the start and finish and takes you from the village of Lenham up to the side of the North Downs and along a stretch of the Pilgrims' Way, perhaps one the most famous long-distance footpaths in the country.

How to get there: Lenham is clearly signed off the A20 between Maidstone and Ashford. From the east leave the M20 at Junction 9, from the west leave at Junction 8. When close to the village and arriving on the A20 from the west ignore the first sign directing HGVs to the Lenham freight depot.
Sat Nav ME17 2PQ.
Parking: There is a car park in the square right in the middle of the village.
OS Map: Explorer 137 Ashford. **Grid ref:** TQ898521.

THE PUB

THE RED LION is a classic friendly local pub with a traditional log fire for cooler days and a beer garden with barbeque area. It retains many of its original 14th-century characteristics with low heavily beamed ceilings throughout. When we walked in a local couple (with a lovely staffi-collie cross) immediately

Terrain: A little road walking in the village to start with but then along paths and tracks through open fields on the slope of the Downs. The busy A20 road has to be crossed twice.
Livestock: None encountered.
Stiles: None.
Nearest vets: Harrietsham Vets, Unit 9, Roebuck Business Park, Ashford Rd, Harrietsham, Maidstone, ME17 1AB. ☎ 01622 858666.

started chatting to us as they'd remembered us having seen us out walking earlier in the day!
⊕ redlionlenham.co.uk ☎ 01622 858531
Also in the square is the aptly named **DOG AND BEAR HOTEL** which has a dog friendly bar area and a fine courtyard garden. Ales are from the Shepherd Neame stable.
⊕ dogandbearlenham.co.uk ☎ 01622 858219

The Walk

1 With your back to whichever pub you have chosen, turn left up Faversham Road passing the old town gaol on the left-hand side. When you get to the busy A20 cross to the other side and turn left. Take the second footpath on the right. Go up the steps and follow the footpath as it bears left diagonally across the field.

2 At the far corner go through the

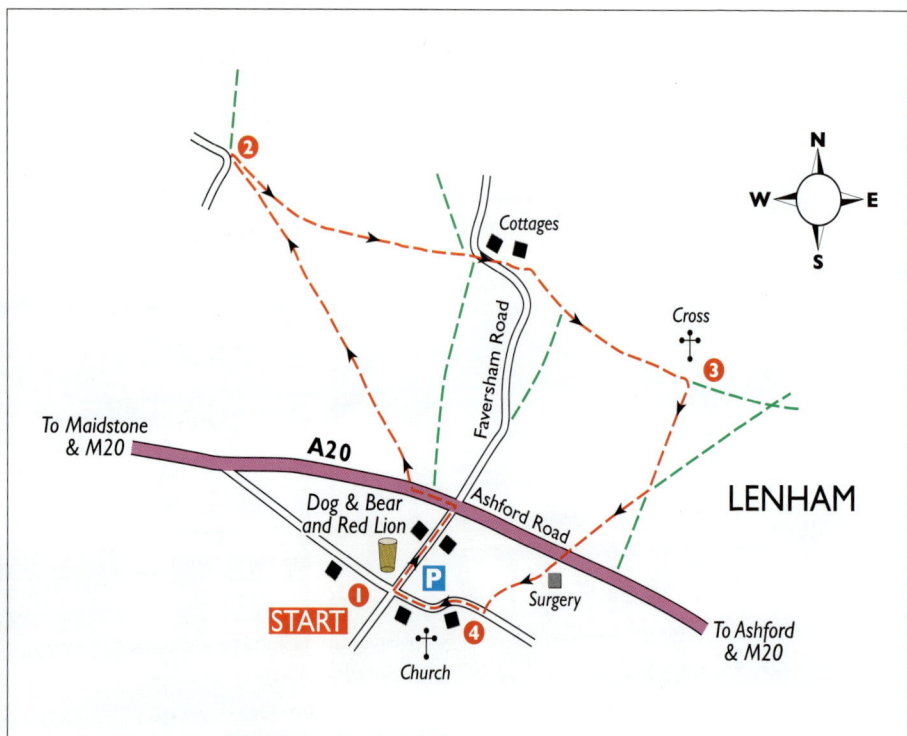

gap in the fence line and turn a sharp dog-leg right. *You are now following the footsteps of pilgrims on the historic route to the shrine of Thomas Becket at Canterbury. From Becket's canonization in 1173, until the Dissolution of the Monasteries in 1538, his shrine became the most important in the country, with claims of 100,000 pilgrims making the journey each year.* You will have views back towards Lenham on your right. Where the track emerges onto a lane for a short distance, keep ahead in the same direction passing some cottages on your left. Where the lane veers right, keep ahead and walk up through the trees. Views of the North Downs ahead of you soon unfold and on your left you will soon be close to a cross carved into the hillside. *The 200-foot chalk cross was dug in 1922 to remember those who fell in the First World War.*

3 From the path below the cross you now turn sharp right along the path dropping back down through the field. About $2/3$ of the way down it is crossed by another path coming diagonally in from the left. Now turn right along this path. If you miss it don't worry, just turn right at the end but it will mean a few metres walking alongside the busy road. Make sure your dog is on a lead and at the end cross the busy A20.

THE
NORTH DOWNS
WAY

FARNHAM
92M

CANTERBURY
21M

DOVER

3 3M

Keep ahead on the other side passing the surgery on the left and community centre on the right. Follow the tarmac path in the same direction beyond the houses.

4 Where the path emerges onto a lane, turn right. Passing the old rectory and church on your left you will soon be back at the square.

12 NEWENDEN
2 miles (3.2 km)

This is one of the shortest walks in the book – perhaps ideal for a quick trip out - but it contains every ingredient of a traditional Kentish walk. The route will take you along footpaths, tracks and quiet lanes, where you'll see some fine views, and finishes with a riverside walk before returning to the dog friendly pub.

How to get there: From the A21 at Flimwell take the A268 signed for Hawkhurst. Continue through Hawkhurst and continue in the same direction when the A28 comes in from the left. Here follow the signpost for Rye and Newenden is a few hundred metres ahead. The pub is on the right-hand side.

Sat Nav TN18 5PN.

Parking: Provided you are a customer of the pub, park at The White Hart. If not, there is limited on-street parking in Lossenham Road opposite.

OS Map: Explorer 125 Romney Marsh, Rye & Winchelsea.

Grid ref: TQ834272.

THE PUB

THE WHITE HART serves good food made with seasonal and locally sourced ingredients. It is also in *CAMRA's Good Beer Guide*. Dogs are welcome in the bar areas.
🌐 thewhitehartnewenden.co.uk
☎ 01797 252166

An alternative is **LIME WHARF CAFÉ** a few metres down the road on the opposite side of the bridge over the river. Based on a Scandinavian boat house design, it is dog friendly and open from 8.30am every day.
🌐 limewharfcafe.co.uk
☎ 01797 253838

Terrain: Apart from the first and last few metres any road walking is along quiet almost deserted lanes. No significant gradients, there is a steady uphill walk through fields near the start of the walk, but nothing too strenuous.
Livestock: None encountered, but note the warning signs about sheep near the river.
Stiles: None.
Nearest vets: Badgers Oak Veterinary Clinic, Hastings Road, Northiam, East Sussex, TN31 6NH. ☎ 01797 252321.

The Walk

1 Turn left with your back to The White Hart pub. Make sure your dog is on a lead and walk a few metres up the pavement taking care as it is narrow outside the pub and the A28 road here can be busy. Take the first right (Beech Road) which is also signed as a public footpath and a few metres further take the footpath on the left. Go through the gap in the fence and up into the field and then follow the path across the field. At the tree line keep ahead following the waymarker. If you look back there are views across the Rother Levels towards Sussex.

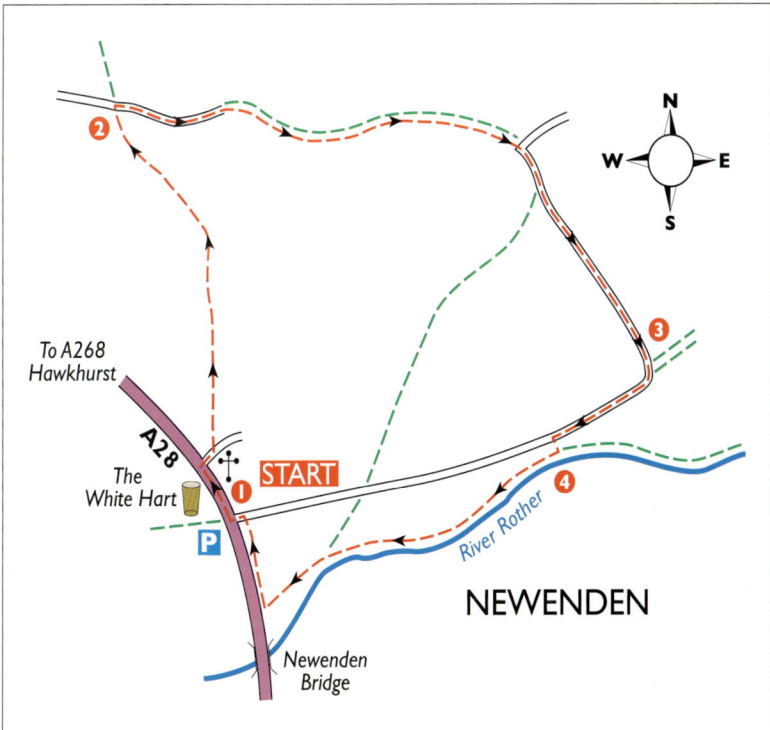

To A268
Hawkhurst

A28

The White Hart

START

P

River Rother

NEWENDEN

Newenden Bridge

2 At the far end take a dog-leg right, along the narrow lane. After a while the tarmac runs out and it becomes a tree-lined bridle path with views opening up on the left, now towards the Kentish Weald. At the far end go through the gate and turn right down the lane.

3 At the bottom of the hill follow the lane round to the right passing an interesting mix of cottages on your right. *Throughout the medieval period, Newenden was a busy inland port until gradual silting of the river meant that it fell out of use in the 16th century. Sea-going ships would leave here heading for London and France. Today you can still take to the river – with your dog – on a 45-minute cruise down the river to Bodiam Castle from the Boat Station next to the bridge.* Take the first footpath on your left, after a few metres this will bring you out on the banks of the River Rother.

4 Turn right and follow the riverside path keeping the river on your left-hand side. When you get to the cricket ground go through the gate and cross to the far left-hand diagonal corner. Turn right at the road to bring you back to The White Hart.

13 PLUCKLEY

4½ miles (7.2 km)

This is a walk based in what is reputedly the most haunted village in the UK. The surrounding area is home to 12 to 16 ghosts, depending on various sources. The Deering family were Lords of the Manor here almost from the time of Henry II and legend has it during the English Civil War the first baronet escaped from Roundhead troops through a narrow, curved-topped window. As a result this type of window was replicated in most of the houses in Pluckley; you will see them everywhere including at The Black Horse.

The route also takes you through a part of the Kentish countryside that became famous in the 1990s when it was the backdrop for many scenes in the television adaptation of the HE Bates novel *The Darling Buds of May*.

How to get there: From the A20 at Charing turn down Station Road. After a few hundred metres the road will become Pluckley Road. Continue for about 5 miles and at Pluckley turn left in the village centre and the pub will be immediately on your left-hand side.
Sat Nav TN27 0QS.
Parking: Park in the village centre outside The Black Horse pub or adjacent to the post office and village stores.
OS Map: Explorer 137 Ashford. **Grid ref:** TQ925454.

THE BLACK HORSE is everything you would expect from a traditional village pub. It boasts beamed ceilings and five log burning fires. It is dog friendly and there is a large garden overlooking the village square. The menu has plenty of pub favourites along with sandwiches and lighter bites for smaller appetites. The pub shares the village reputation for having a ghost, and it is claimed there is an invisible phantom which moves possessions around the pub which can go missing for days on end – although we find much the same problem simply by having a dog!
⊕ blackhorsepluckley.co.uk ☎ 01233 841948

THE SWAN INN at Little Chart has recently been refurbished in a rustic but homely style featuring bare boards and a real fire. There is plenty of outside seating and a riverside garden. The menu specialises in traditional English fare including afternoon and cream teas. Some traditional ales on tap. Usually closed on Mondays.
⊕ swanlittlechartashford.co.uk
☎ 01233 840011

Terrain: A little bit of road walking, then tracks and footpaths. There are a few gradients with the climbs sustained but not too steep.
Livestock: We encountered sheep towards the end of the walk.
Stiles: A few, but all dog friendly.
Nearest vets: Lady Dane Veterinary Centre, Unit 1 The Old Pumping Station, Pluckley Road, Charing, Ashford, TN27 0AH.
☎ 01233 714796.

The Walk

1 Turn right outside The Black Horse pub and at the T junction cross the road turning right up the path on the left-hand side of the road as it climbs the hill. Follow this path a few metres until you reach the steps dropping down to the right following the car park and footpath sign. Continue a few metres towards the car park but then take the gate on the left into the recreation ground. Keep to the right-hand side and you will see a gap in the bushes next to a grassed children's play area. Follow this path which emerges onto a broad track with orchards firstly on the left and then the right-hand side. Keep ahead across the tarmac drive. A little further on, the path goes slightly left and right before crossing a lane. At the lane keep going ahead with a high wall on the left-hand side. You will cross several stiles and a sunken dip. After the sunken dip keep ahead across the broad field, follow it through the next tree line and right to the very bottom. You will emerge onto a further large field with a modern church prominently on your left-hand side. *The new Little Chart parish church is dedicated to Saint Mary the Virgin, and built in 1955. It replaced Little Chart's former parish church, parts of which dated back to Norman times. On 16 August 1944, it was destroyed when it received a direct hit from a German flying bomb, with only the badly damaged 15th-century tower and parts of the chancel wall surviving. The bells from the old church were recovered and were used to cast the bells that now hang in the new church.* In the middle of this field there is a crossroads of paths. If you have gone further than the church on the left-hand side you have missed the turn. At the crossroads of paths turn left. Follow the path down to the left-hand side of the church and out

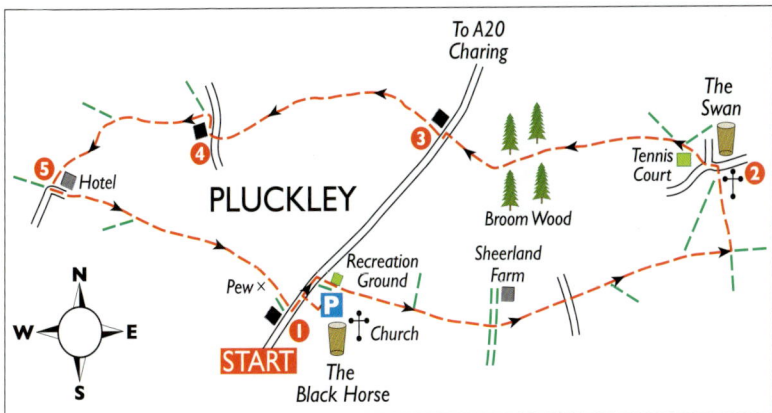

onto the road where you will now be opposite The Swan Inn. Cross the road.

❷ Passing the pub on your right-hand side, cross the road to the side of the pub and take the footpath facing you. Pass the tennis court on the left-hand side and take the path with the hedge line on your right-hand side. A short distance later you will come to a footpath waymarker sign. Now take the path that diverges left across the field. Keep ahead across the field to the far side where the path enters Broom Wood. Continue to the far side of the wood. At the gate at the end, bear right across the field. You will be heading towards the house on the right-hand side on the horizon. At the end go through the gate and turn left down the road for a few metres. Take the next footpath on the right next to the signpost for Jennings Farm.

❸ Follow the drive with houses on both sides until the end. Go through the gate. With the end of the drive still on your right-hand side, keep ahead following the footpath waymarker up a few steps next to a tree. Continue ahead across the next field. Go through the gate at the end. Now follow the path up the field, bearing slightly left to the very end. To your right there are fine views of Egerton church in the distance and the North Downs.

❹ At the far end of the field cross the road and go down the lane opposite. Follow this as it twists and turns. It soon becomes an unmade trackway. Do not cross the stile ahead of you but follow the track as it veers left with the valley dropping to your right-hand side. Follow the winding track as it eventually drops down the hillside.

❺ Where the track emerges onto a road, turn sharp left passing Elvey Farm Hotel on the left-hand side. Continue past the front of the hotel and go through the gate ahead of you. At the other side of the gate keep to the broader right-hand track across the field. You now follow the blue waymarkers and you will see Pluckley village and the top of the church ahead of you at the top of the hill in the distance. You now just keep ahead in the same direction following the blue waymarkers through several gates up the hillside. Near the top you will see a perching bench inviting you to 'take a pew and enjoy the view'. After this follow the path as it bears right behind a modernist house on the right-hand side. Go through the gate facing you and at the end of the drive turn left up the hill into the village. You will be back at the start a few metres later.

14 SANDGATE

5 miles (8 km)

This walk features the story of defending the realm at the time of threatened Napoleonic invasion, but given the number and different types of watering holes along the way, it could also be a bit of a coastal pub crawl – and all dog friendly! We take in a length of the coast between Sandgate and Hythe with a long walk along the seafront promenade on the way out and a tranquil canalside return.

How to get there: From Folkestone town centre follow the signs for A259 Hythe. This will take you through Sandgate High Street. The Sandgate Hotel is on your right-hand side shortly after the road has met the sea.
Sat Nav CT20 3DY.
Parking: There is free on-street parking at the start on the left-hand side of the road. Spaces may get taken quickly during the day so there is an alternative start point in a pay and display car park a few hundred metres into the walk itself.
OS Map: Explorer 138 Dover, Folkestone & Hythe.
Grid ref: TR196350.

THE PUB

THE SANDGATE HOTEL is stylish and modern and includes a dog friendly bar featuring a coal fire by winter and a fantastic sunny terrace overlooking the English Channel during the summer. A great place to sit and watch the world go by. Water bowls are provided.
🌐 sandgatehotel.com ☎ 01303 220444

THE POTTING SHED is a former café that has been converted into a micropub at the east end of Hythe High Street. It has simple décor, dogs are welcome but children less so. Closed on Mondays.
☎ 07780 877226

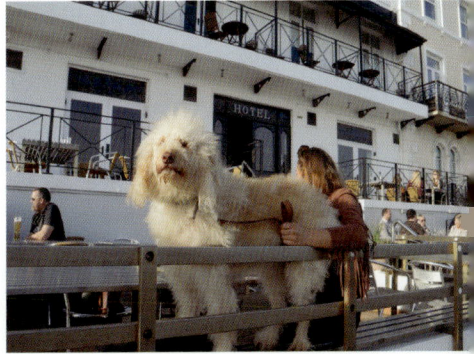

THE INN DOORS is at the west end of Sandgate. It is a micropub based upon a 1930s living room consisting of a small bar and two-level seating. Four Ales are served by gravity from a cold room and on our last visit it was Gin Night with over 70 different varieties available!
⊕ inndoorsmicropub.co.uk ☎ 07958 474473

THE PROVIDENCE INN is a more traditional pub at the further end of Sandgate High Street if you're looking for something simpler.
☎ 01303 249962

The Walk

• •

❶ With your back to the hotel, cross the road and turn right along the esplanade. Depending on the time of year you have the choice of walking along the beach, although various sections are subject to dog control orders between May and September so you will need to check the signs as you go along. After a short distance the promenade separates from the road. Once the main A259 road has peeled off to the right you will have the long and wide Princes Parade stretching into the distance. You now follow this promenade all the way until you reach Hythe. After approximately a 1½ miles you will pass the Imperial Hotel on the right-hand side. Where the road swings inland keep ahead along the promenade. *Following the French Revolution, Napoleon declared war on Britain in 1793. To counter the threat, a line of forts and towers were built along the coast. The towers were based on a round*

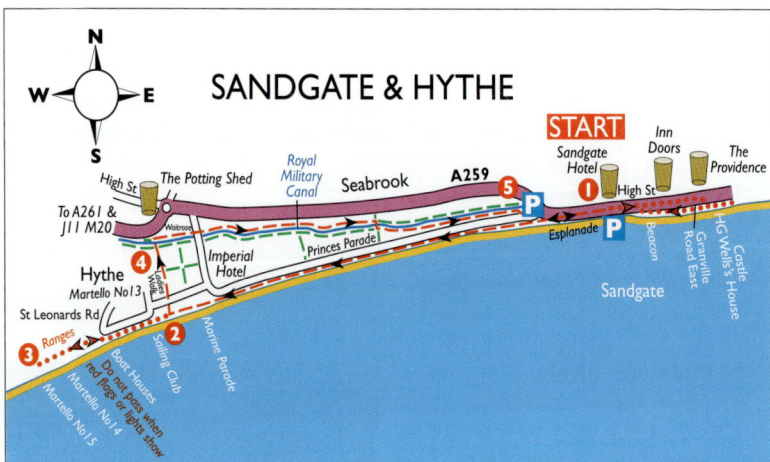

tower at Cape Mortella in Corsica. 'Mortella' became 'Martello' and 74 of them were built between Folkestone and Seaford between 1805 and 1810. The walls are 13 feet thick on the seaward side but only 7 feet thick on the less vulnerable landward side.

2 Just before you reach the sailing club you have a choice. You can continue ahead to take a close look at three Martello towers, or alternatively turn right here down Moyle Tower Road for the main walk. If you want to take a closer look keep ahead along the promenade. However, there are occasions when firing ranges behind the towers are in use and if red flags or lights are showing in the distance you cannot take up this option. If you are continuing, shortly after another road swings in from the right you will see the white painted Martello Tower Number 13 which was converted into a house in 1928. Continue along West Parade and where it swings inland at St Leonard's Road, drop down to the beach and keep ahead in the same direction. You need to be aware that this is a working beach and although public have access it is home to Hythe's fishing fleet and you need to take particular care of machinery and especially of the low slung hawsers which are strung along the beach.

After a few hundred metres you will come to the Hythe military range boundary. If the red flags or lights are showing at the boundary you cannot proceed any further. If it is clear continue ahead and take the path behind the two Martello towers you can see in front of you.

3 Returning to point 2 now turn left after the sailing club. Cross the road and take Ladies Walk directly ahead of you.

4 Once you have crossed the canal bridge you have another choice. If you have worked up enough thirst for a drink, continue ahead and turn right at the main road, follow it round and at the roundabout turn left and a few metres down the high street on the left-hand side you will find the Potting Shed micro pub. To continue with the walk at point 4 turn sharp right after you have crossed the canal. *The Royal Military Canal was another defence to Napoleonic Invasion.* You now have a pleasant 1½ mile walk along the canal banks. With a path on both sides it doesn't really matter which side you are on. There are several bridges which you can cross and recross at will. However, towards the end you need to be on the right-hand bank as this will make leaving the canal easier at its far eastern end.

5 When you do reach the end take the steps up to the car park, cross it and the road and turn left and you will be back on Sandgate esplanade. Retrace your steps back to the start point. However, if you wish to try a couple of other pubs, continue along the road. After a while you will have the Inn Doors on the left and shortly after that the more traditional Providence on the right. The Ship Inn does not allow dogs on the premises. To return back, after the Providence, turn right down Granville Road East passing HG Wells's House at the end on the left. Once you are on the esplanade turn right for a beach-side walk back to point 1.

15 SANDWICH

4½ miles (7.2 km)

This contrasting walk takes you from the historic Cinque Port of Sandwich across the courses of the Royal St George's Golf Club to the sea, along a quiet stretch of beach and back alongside the scenic meanders of the River Stour.

Sandwich is claimed to be the most complete medieval town in England. It is also where the sandwich was invented. In 1762, John Montagu, 4th Earl of Sandwich, asked for meat to be served between slices of bread to avoid interrupting his card game.

How to get there: From the A256 follow the directions to Sandwich town centre and the quay. The car park is at the quay next to the bridge over the River Stour.
Sat Nav CT13 9EN.
Parking: In the public car park by the quay in Sandwich.
OS Map: Explorer 150 Canterbury & Isle of Thanet.
Grid ref: TR332582.

THE CRISPIN INN was built in 1491, and was for many years an ordinary house. In 1769 a licence was granted to sell ales from the premises. It later became known as the 'Crispin' after St Crispin who was said to have been shipwrecked in the English Channel near Sandwich. With a bar adorned with hops, this pub retains the charm of a Kentish pub. There is a patio next to the river. Our dog was spoilt by the barman with a dog biscuit in front of the open fire! Real ale includes two house beers brewed locally.

🌐 sandwichpubs.co.uk

☎ 01304 621967

The Walk

. . . .

1 Go to the far end of the car park furthest away from the bridge. Take the broad drive through the park. Continue along the shared path with the cycle way alongside the river. Turn left at the first metal bridge over the river and follow the path bearing slightly right then left.

2 You will shortly come to a junction of paths. Carry on straight ahead following the Saxon Shore Way marker. You now follow this all the way to the sea. About half way along you will cross a small road with the Royal St George's Golf Club on the right-hand side. After this you will be crossing the golf course. *Founded in 1887 and intended to be a South of England rival to St Andrew's, St George's is ranked amongst the leading courses in the world. In 1894 the first Open Championship played outside of Scotland was played here. The course has hosted the Open on fourteen occasions. The club's Challenge Trophy, dating from 1888 is one of the oldest trophies in golf.* It's quite a privilege to be able to wander across this historic course with your dog so take care to follow the white signs and watch out for golf balls.

Terrain: Flat and easy with no road walking.
Livestock: None.
Stiles: None.
Nearest vets: White Mill Vets, Ash Road, Sandwich, Kent, CT13 9JB.
☎ 01304 611 999.

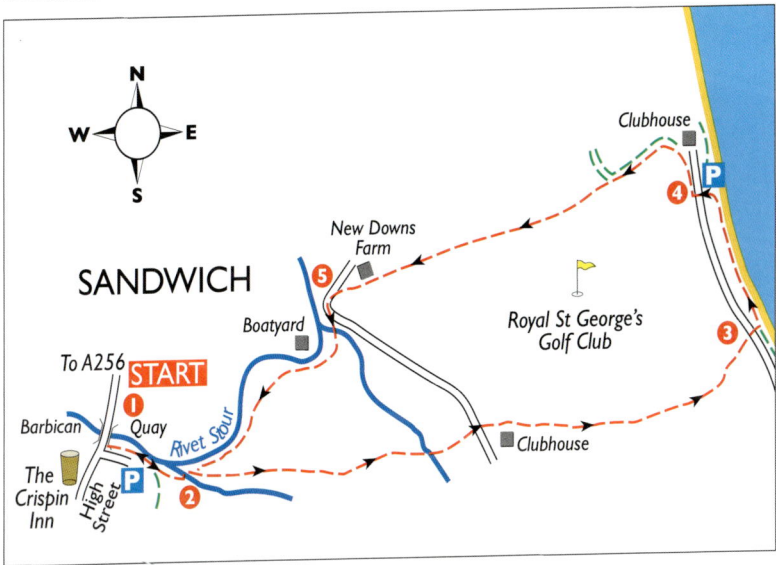

3 When you get to the beach, cross the road and bear left and continue your walk in the direction of the white clubhouse in the distance. When you reach the car park, cut through it to the white entrance gates to the club house.

4 The footpath runs along the grass on the left side of the drive leading up to the clubhouse. Just before you reach the club house, bear left and take the track heading back across the golf course. After a short while the track veers right but the footpath keeps going ahead. You are now on the Stour Valley Walk. Follow this until you skirt New Downs Farm on your right-hand side. Please note that just before you get to the farm you will notice a stile in a fence line on the right-hand side. Do not go over this, but instead keep going ahead until you reach a road.

5 At the road go through the gate and turn left. A few metres later keep ahead where the road veers to the left. Follow the Stour Valley Walk footpath sign keeping the substation on your left and you will soon have the River Stour on your right. Carry on along the raised path next to the river and this will bring you back to point 2. Turn right to retrace your steps to the start. If you want to explore the town head through the barbican gate and up the High Street.

16 SHOREHAM & POLHILL
4 miles (6.4 km)

This is one of our favourite walks and it is packed with variety and things to see. It takes in the picturesque village of Shoreham as well as several viewpoints where you can admire far-reaching views across the Darenth Valley and the Vale of Holmesdale. Part of the route passes through a nature reserve and includes stretches along hillsides, through woodlands (which are carpeted with bluebells in spring) and next to a small river in the village.

How to get there: From the M25 Junction 3/M20 Junction 1 follow the A20 signed to Farningham. At the second roundabout keep ahead but take the next right turn (A225). After 4 miles take the right-hand turn signposted for Shoreham. Go under the railway bridge and follow the road through the village. At the far end turn left and the car park is a few metres further on the left-hand side. **Sat Nav TN14 7SR**.

Parking: There is no large car park at the pub and whilst on-street parking around the village is mostly unrestricted there is a real issue of inconsiderate parking obstructing the flow of traffic in some places. For this reason we recommend parking in the free car park off Filston Lane. It's only a few metres from the walk itself so we have made it the start and finish point.

OS Map: Explorer 147 Sevenoaks & Tonbridge. **Grid ref:** TQ518615.

Terrain: A little bit of road walking in the village at the start and finish, otherwise footpaths and tracks. There are a couple of quite steep gradients. The tracks through Pilots Wood and Meenfield Wood are muddy in winter.
Livestock: Sometimes between point 5 and the bottom of the hill.
Stiles: Only one and it is dog friendly.
Nearest vets: Sevenoaks Veterinary Surgery, 104 Seal Rd, Sevenoaks, TN14 5AU. ☎ 01732 740999.

THE PUB **YE OLDE GEORGE INN** is one of four pubs in the village. There are low beams, uneven floors and, in winter, cosy fires. Dogs are welcome in the bar and in the back room. Some of the ales are from local breweries. In the summer you can sit at the picnic benches at the front of the pub.
☎ 01959 522017

THE CROWN is at the other end of the village between points 5 and 6 on the walk and allows dogs in certain parts of the bar area.
☎ 01959 522903
The Two Brewers in the middle of the village no longer welcomes dogs.

The Walk

1 Walk out of the car park and turn right into Filston Lane. Take the next left up The Landway, also signed as a public footpath. Carry on up the hill. Just after the steepest part, where there are some steps, you will come to a crossroads of paths. Turn left and take the path with the valley on your left-hand side. There are some great views looking back down at the village with vistas right and left along the Darenth Valley. Continue along this path until you reach a gate where the path emerges into a field.

2 Go through the gate. There is another good view point with a bench a couple of metres up the hill on your right-hand side. Continuing with the walk, cross straight across the field and go through the dog friendly stile on the far side. Keep along this path with the field line to your right and continue ahead where a broader path joins from the right. You now follow this broader path as it twists and turns through the woods. At the end you will be facing a path with a stile to your left and spaced wooden steps to the right. Turn right here up the steps and go through the gate. The path climbs steadily uphill

(don't take the broader track that diverges left). You will pass through a few gates and hedgerows until you reach a small bench on the left-hand side just before the path heads up into the woods.

3 *The view is of Polhill Bank Nature Reserve, managed by the Kent Wildlife Trust. The 'Bank' is almost four hectares of chalk grassland on this southeast-facing hillside.*

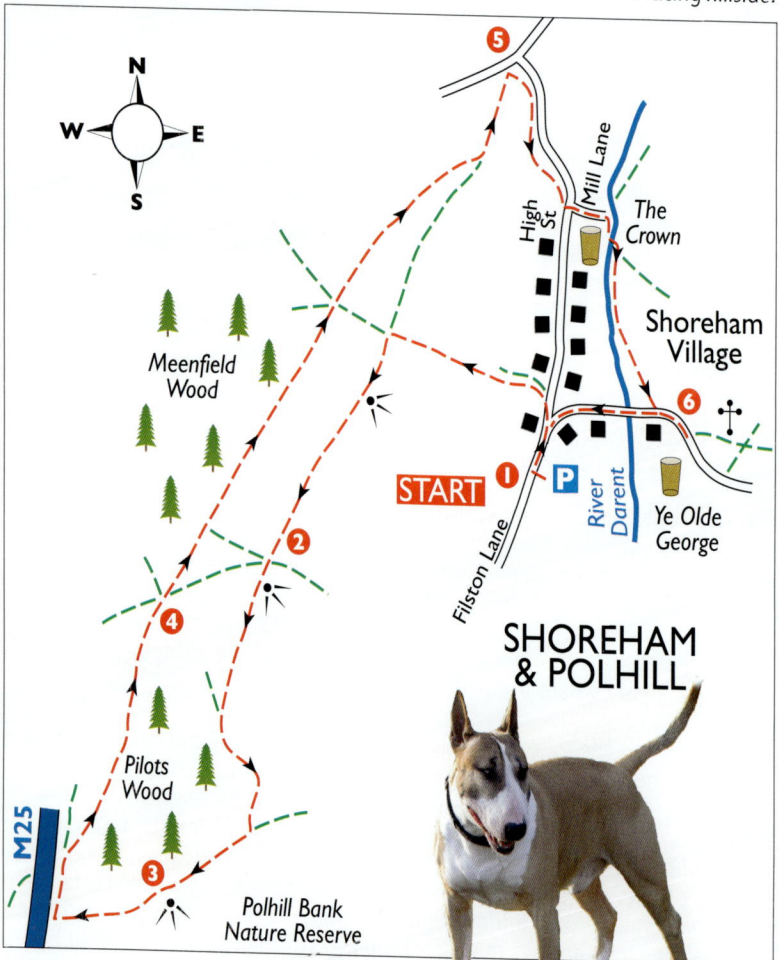

The railway line you can see on the right is the main line from Dover to London. Occasionally you might be lucky enough to see a special train headed by a steam locomotive pounding its way up the gradient before disappearing into the tunnel almost beneath your feet. Carry on up the path which now heads uphill through the woods. Follow it as it turns right. You now have a less welcome form of transport in the form of the M25 directly below you on your left-hand side. Don't worry, there is a good fence protecting the path from the drop down to the road. Where there is a footbridge over the motorway on your left, keep ahead up a few steps continuing in the same direction. A few metres later bear right along the footpath into the woods. There are a few peripheral paths here but they all head in the same direction. You are now in Pilots Wood. There are good carpets of bluebells here around the end of April/beginning of May. You carry along the broadening track through the woods in the same direction.

4 You will emerge at a rough crossroads of five paths. Bear right keeping to the broadest track with the hedge line on your right-hand side. Don't go through the stile on the right into the field. Keep ahead along this track which will soon enter Meenfield. You now just keep ahead along the track, going straight ahead at another

crossroads of five paths. After a steepish descent another path will join from the right. Carry on in the same direction.

5 At the end of the path, where it turns left towards a road, turn right and drop down the hill and go through the gate. Keep to the path on the left-hand side of the field which will bring you out at the bottom of the hill opposite Mill Lane. The Crown Inn is a few metres along the High Street on the right. To continue the walk, carry on down Mill Lane with its collection of old village cottages. At the bottom turn right past Mill House and cross the river. Immediately after the bridge turn right and follow the river bank. Although looking quiet and peaceful, the river here can be deceptively fast flowing so it's worth exercising a bit of care – we nearly ended up with a dog following his ball into the current here! Follow the riverside path, after it veers slightly away from the river you have the impressive Water House on the left, associated with the 19th-century artist Samuel Palmer. *Shoreham boasts a wealth of old houses, both grand and small. Quintessential English cottages are around every corner. The village flourished in Georgian times, when many fine houses were built near the river including Water House. Some of the houses are marked with suns – the mark of the insurance company. Paid-for firefighters would only attend fires at homes with the appropriate sign. It is claimed that the inspiration for the words of William Blake's hymn 'Jerusalem' came from the countryside around the village.* You will soon come to the war memorial and bridge on your right-hand side and next to the bridge the old ford across the river. Follow the road around to the left and Ye Olde George Inn will be a few metres further up on the right-hand side.

6 Retrace your steps from the pub but this time cross the river, at the end of the road turn left and the car park will be on your left.

17 TANKERTON & WHITSTABLE
4 miles (6.4 km)

This is one of the best walks in the county with two pubs, a clifftop stroll, a traditional beach hut-lined promenade to walk along plus a year-round dog friendly beach. There is also the chance to slightly extend the walk and take a look around one of the most charismatic and popular seaside towns in the country. There is something for everyone here.

How to get there: From the A299 take the exit for Whitstable. Continue along the B2205 through the town centre following the signs for Tankerton. Turn left up the hill into Tower Hill. This will lead into Marine Parade where there is plenty of unrestricted parking. The Royal pub is towards the far end on the right-hand side.
Sat Nav CT5 2BB.
Parking: There is plenty of unrestricted parking along Marine Parade in Tankerton.
OS Map: Explorer 150 Canterbury & Isle of Thanet.
Grid ref: TR124672.

THE ROYAL is situated upon the top of the Tankerton Slopes and offers sea views. The bar is surprisingly modern and although dogs are restricted to the bar area, you are able to order food from the restaurant to eat in the bar.

🌐 royaltankerton.co.uk ☎ 01227 272008

THE TANKERTON ARMS is set back one block from the clifftop in Tankerton's main shopping street. This is a micro pub; you will find no lagers and spirits, no music, cooked food, television or gaming machines. Drinks, including a selection of 6 or so real ales, wine and soft drinks are served personally at the tables. Whilst dogs are allowed, mobile phones and music are not! Usually closed on Mondays.

🌐 thetankertonarms.co.uk ☎ 07532 025626

Terrain: Seaside promenade, well marked footpaths and the broad grassy swathes of Tankerton Slopes. If you choose to walk a little bit further into Whitstable there will be a short distance along a fairly busy road. Apart from one slight incline, the route is flat.

Livestock: None.

Stiles: None.

Nearest vets: Broadway Vet Group, 1 The Broadway, Herne Bay, CT6 8SR. ☎ 01227 375978.

The Walk

1 With your back to The Royal walk out onto the broad grassy area in front of you. Turn to the right. Continue, enjoying fine sea views on your left and distant views of Herne Bay with its forlorn and isolated pier head marooned out at sea ahead of you. *The slopes between where you are walking and the beach are home to Hog's Fennel, one of Britain's rarest plants and two equally rare moths! On a clear day you can see Southend-on-Sea across the estuary together with the historic Maunsell wartime sea forts at the mouth of the River Thames.* Pass the Sea View Café on the right-hand side as the slope gently drops down towards the sea. Where at the end Marine Crescent peters out, take the path a few metres on your left and then turn immediately right behind the beach huts. Then turn right onto the promenade for a short distance.

2 Turn right a few metres later at the sign pointing inland signed Oyster Bay Trail Herne Bay. Follow this raised path as it forms a near semi-circle with marshland on your left and views of the little church on your right. At the far end you will be facing the sea.

3 Turn left to walk parallel along the sea front. *This stretch is known as Long Rock and has been designated part of the Thanet coast Site of Special Scientific Interest. Important bird populations gather on the shingle beach here to feed and breed and the grassland supports rare plants and insects. The brook that you cross has a small population of water voles.* You now walk along the promenade but can stop off for a run on the beach should you so wish. This end of Tankerton beach provides unrestricted dog access all year round. Continue along the promenade with the colourful beach huts on your left until you finally round the headland, pass Beacon House and Whitstable harbour comes into view.

4 At this point on your right-hand side there is a long shingle spit known

TANKERTON & WHITSTABLE

as Whitstable Street which is uncovered only at the lowest tide. Once you have gone through the large metal barriers you will come to the start of the road known as Beach Walk. If you wish to continue into Whitstable town, continue ahead and at the end turn right into Harbour Street taking care as it is quite a busy road. As soon as you have the chance, turn right into the harbour area next to the harbour offices. Bear left with the quayside on your right-hand side and follow the harbour round to the right. You now have a choice of where you wish to go to explore this characterful seaside town.

5 *For ever associated with oysters, it has been dubbed the Pearl of Kent. There is the quayside, beachfront, bustling harbour and quaint side streets with names such as Squeeze Gut Alley to explore. It has a working harbour where you can watch the boats come in or take a walk along the beachfront path. There is no shortage of pubs either, if you are on the seafront you'll see the famous Neptune, situated right on the beach ahead of you, and it is dog friendly.* To return to the main walk, at the bottom of Beach Walk just after the public toilets, take a sharp dog-leg left up the hill. A few metres up the hill on the right-hand side there is a tea house with garden seating which is open in the summer months. Continue up the path and through the trees then take the steps in front of you which will bring you back out onto the top of Tankerton Slopes. Keep to the left along the green and after a while you will see The Royal on your right-hand side.

18 WESTBERE & FORDWICH

3½ miles (5.6 km)

The phrase 'best kept secret' is often overused, but this walk explores a village and town which really do fit the bill. Westbere is a tiny Kentish village and it's just off the main Canterbury to Thanet road, the lane passing through the village is lined with houses reflecting a diversity of hundreds of years of history.

How to get there: From Canterbury take the A28 signposted to Margate. After the level crossing at Sturry, follow the road round to the right. A ½ mile later, look out for a sign to turn right for 'Westbere Village only'. The pub is in the centre of the village on the right-hand side.
Sat Nav CT2 0HH.
Parking: Park considerately in Westbere village, or if visiting Ye Olde Yew Tree Inn, then use the car park there with permission.
OS Map: Explorer 150 Canterbury & Isle of Thanet.
Grid ref: TR193610.

THE PUB **YE OLDE YEW TREE INN** started life as a 14th-century hall house. It is reputed to have become a pub about 200 years ago. It has a multitude of claims; to be the oldest pub in Kent, that Queen Anne and the Archbishop of Canterbury have stayed there, that a pair of ghosts are in residence and that Dick Turpin evaded capture from the law hiding out here. What is beyond doubt is that its heavily beamed interior boasts one of the most magnificent inglenook fireplaces for miles around. There is also a large beer garden at the back. Real ales from independent Kentish breweries are well kept and the food receives good reviews.

⊕ yewtreewestbere.co.uk ☎ 01227 710501

THE GEORGE & DRAGON is right next to the River Stour at Fordwich and is another pub with a long history. Today it has been smartly refurbished and offers a good menu and local ales. There are pleasant seating areas away from the bar where you can eat from the restaurant menu.

⊕ homecountiespubs.co.uk/georgeanddragon ☎ 01227 710661

Terrain: Footpaths and broad tracks with a short distance of road walking in the quiet village and later 80 yards on a pavement in Fordwich. No gradients.
Livestock: None.
Stiles: None.
Nearest vets: Broadway Veterinary Group, 37 Hoades Wood Road, Sturry, Canterbury, Kent, CT2 0LY. ☎ 01227 713390.

The Walk

1 With your back to Ye Olde Yew Tree Inn turn left through the village along Westbere Lane. *As you follow the walk you'll see Kemp Hall house on the right-hand side which is a medieval hall house where the timber-framed parts date from around 1480. Further along on the right is Westbere House which has its origins in the early 1700s. Passing the village green on the right-hand side you will also pass Cecil Cottages on the left dating from 1881.* Where the lane turns to the right take the narrow footpath on the left. This will open out into woods. Follow it

down to the railway line and continue ahead with the railway parallel on your left-hand side. There is pleasant woodland on your right although this will later give way to fencing when you reach the back gardens of the village of Sturry. At the far end of the path, go through the gate and cross the railway line. Go through the trees and you will find a miniature railway circuit facing you.

2 Turn right along the track with the miniature railway on your left. Follow it on your left as it goes round the corner with a football field on your right. You will soon come to a broad private road. Turn right along this road. This is also a public footpath. Towards the end don't worry if you turn the corner and see the large metal security gates shut and blocking the road. A small gap has been provided on the right-hand side to keep the footpath right of way open. You need to be aware of the occasional lorry on this road as it is a private drive serving an aggregate depot. When you come to the end, turn left at the main road. Continue on the pavement for 70 metres.

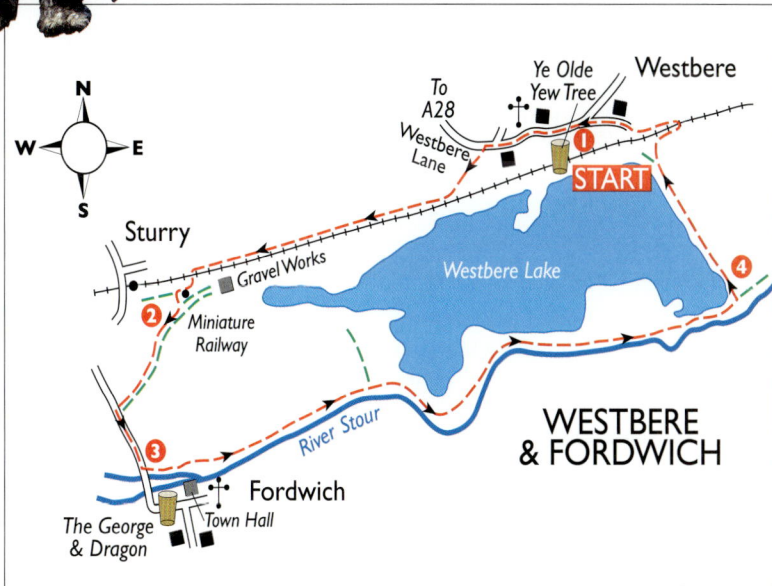

3 When you come to the Fordwich town sign you can keep ahead and cross the bridge to explore historic Fordwich. The George & Dragon pub is a few metres on the other side of the second bridge. For the walk do not cross the bridge but turn left following the public footpath sign. You will soon have a good view of Fordwich church and the old town hall across the river on your right-hand side. You now follow the riverside path for about a mile. You will glimpse Westbere Lake on your left-hand side. This is a charming riverside walk alongside the River Stour. *It's so peaceful today, but for 2,000 years this was the only route to transport heavy goods to Canterbury. It's amazing to think of it today but every Caen stone used by the Normans to rebuild Canterbury Cathedral in the 12th and 13th centuries was floated along the river past this spot and offloaded at Fordwich.* You will be taking a left turn away from the river. Ignore the left-hand path next to a bench and also ignore the many little paths for anglers which branch left heading to Westbere Lake. Once the woodland on the far side of the river on your right has given way to open fields, be ready to take the first broad track (not small footpath) on your left-hand side.

4 Take this turn, keeping Westbere Lake on your left-hand side. At this point the lake will be very close to the footpath. Continue along the broad track. Where it emerges into a slight clearing in front of the houses follow the yellow waymarker right; this smaller path is the public right of way. You will shortly find the railway line in front of you. You will need to turn right along the new path as the crossing has been moved further along to improve sight lines on the railway. Cross the railway lines and double back along the path turning right at the cottage and then bear left up Walnut Tree Lane. At the far end turn left and Ye Olde Yew Tree Inn will be on the left-hand side.

19 THE WHITE CLIFFS

6 miles (9.6 km)

The White Cliffs of Dover are one of the most iconic symbols of Britain; the towering chalk, a symbol of home and also of wartime defence. There is lots to see on this walk with stunning views and reminders of a wartime past at every turn. The route is one of our favourites and takes you from Dover to St Margaret's Bay and back. Highlights also include a break at a famous lighthouse and a pub stop at a picturesque bay.

How to get there: From Ashford/London on the A20 drop down to the seafront. At the far end turn left turn into Woolcomber Street at the traffic lights signed for Dover Castle. At the next set of traffic lights you'll see a National Trust sign pointing uphill, keep going past the castle entrance. When you get to the top of the hill there is another brown sign opposite the entrance into Upper Road. The car park entrance is 1 mile further down Upper Road, at the sharp bend in the road.
Sat Nav CT15 5NA.
Parking: At the National Trust White Cliffs visitor centre. Free to National Trust members.
OS Map: Explorer 138 Dover, Folkestone and Hythe.
Grid ref: TR335422.

Terrain: Undulating as the route keeps to the rise and fall of the cliffs. There is one quite steep descent down steps and several climbs, but well worth the effort. Only a few metres of road walking throughout.
Livestock: Grazing horses beyond point 2 on the outward walk.
Stiles: None.
Nearest vets: Burnham House Veterinary Surgery, 33-35 Castle St, Dover, CT16 1PT. ☎ 01304 206989.

THE PUB **COASTGUARD** is Britain's nearest pub to France and sits in an enviable position with great views over St Margaret's Bay and the sea. It has recently been taken over by Shepherd Neame and branded with a significant nautical theme with a large window at the front engraved with the Plimsoll Line, and porthole-style decorations around the pub. Dogs are welcome inside and out with water bowls on the terrace. At the foot of the cliffs you will have lost your UK mobile phone signal – the signal here comes from France!
⊕ thecoastguard.co.uk ☎ 01304 853051

The Walk

. . . .

❶ To start the walk, go through the gate at the far end of the car park. Where the paths immediately divide take the left-hand fork. If you turn round you can get some good views of Dover Castle on the opposite hilltop. Go through the next gate, follow the purple waymarker and take the right-hand fork. The path will drop down and meet another path coming in from the right. Turn left here. At the bottom of the next set of steps you will come to a junction of paths.

❷ Keep ahead in the same direction taking the wide cinder track which starts to head uphill. At the top go through the gate and turn right along the track. You now keep ahead along this track all the way to the South Foreland lighthouse which you can see in the distance. *The current lighthouse was built in 1843, to mark the dangerous offshore banks of the Goodwin Sands known as the 'swallower of ships'. In 1858 it became the first lighthouse to show an electric lantern and more significantly in 1898 Marconi*

demonstrated the first ever ship-to-shore message from the East Goodwin lightship and a year later the first international radio transmission in the world from Wimereux, in France. As you pass the lighthouse the entrance is on the right-hand side if you wish to have a closer look or take a refreshment stop if the 1950s-themed Mrs Knotts tearoom is open (check the signs outside). Dogs are only allowed at the outside tables.

3 A few metres further on behind the lighthouse a metal gate opens onto a crossroad where a footpath crosses the track. Turn left here following the path along the edge of the woods. At the far end turn right along the track. *The coastline around Dover was known as hellfire corner during the Second World War being massively defended and fortified with coastal artillery, extensive tunnels and radar installations. On this walk you will often come across concrete or metal remains all of which have significance from this era. The track here was built to service some of the biggest guns the world had seen, capable of landing shells across the Channel in France.* You now keep ahead along this track. After some time it will become a very quiet residential

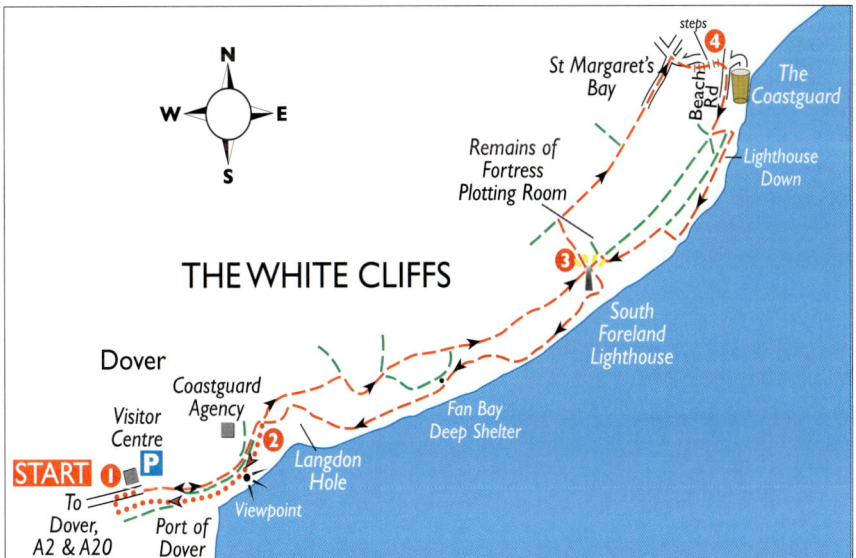

THE WHITE CLIFFS

Dover

road. At the end of the road turn right. After a few metres, when you come to the first side road on the right, take the footpath that drops down parallel to the main road signposted 'steps to beach'. There is now a long descent down these steps through the woods to the bottom of the cliff. When you reach the bottom turn left.

4 You now have a very short distance along a road with no pavement but this will very quickly bring you out at the seafront right next to Coastguard.

Returning from the pub, retrace your steps to point 4. Now keep ahead and almost immediately take the left turn into Beach Road, pass the entrance to the Pines Garden on your right and the small museum and tea room on your left. Carry on up the hill and follow the road which eventually becomes an unmade track. Take the dog-leg left following the Saxon Shore Way footpath sign. The track will climb further uphill but when it turns right keep ahead taking the footpath up a few steps and through a gate marked with the National Trust 'Lighthouse Down' sign. Once you have gone through the gate bear right keeping the clifftop on your left. Follow either path to the far end and then bear right when it approaches a small patch of wooded scrub. Don't follow the smaller path into the trees. Having followed the path round to the right it will bring you up to a gate and onto a lane. Go through the gate and turn left up the lane. In a short while the lighthouse will be visible in front of you. Where the lane comes to a rough crossroad, turn left up to the lighthouse. Immediately on your right-hand side there is a gate leading into the wood. This leads a few metres further on to the remains of the Second

World War gun fortress plotting room which was the command centre for all the local gun batteries. There is an information board which will give you more detail. Back on the main path, a few metres later you will be back at the gate at point 3.

Now turn left, skirting the lighthouse on your right and follow the path to the clifftop, then turn right along the coast path. You now follow this path all the way back in the direction of Dover until you get back to point 2.

Here you have a choice, you can climb the steps and retrace your outward route, or you can bear left and take the broad lower route but beware that if you take the lower route, further ahead there is a very narrow path right next to a steep unfenced drop. If you are taking the lower route, on your left-hand side you will have a fine view of Langdon Bay. Continue along the wide grassy track but you then take the narrow footpath on your right which climbs back up the cliff side. Be very careful here given the steep drop on the left-hand side. At the end go through the gate, then bear right, cross the grassy area and you will be back close to the entrance of the visitor centre. Turn right along the entrance road and you will be back at the start.

20 WORMSHILL
2½ miles (4 km)

This is a walk through pleasant but quite remote countryside that few people actually stop to visit. It's on some of the highest ground in the county with the occasional view right across to the Isle of Sheppey. The village contains a number of heritage-listed buildings, which include a Norman church, a 17th-century pub, the second oldest surviving post office building in the UK and a Victorian pillar box said to be the oldest in the county.

How to get there: From the M20 Junction 8 follow the signs for Lenham. After you have left the interchange roundabout take the left at the second roundabout signposted Hollingbourne B2163. Continue up Hollingbourne Hill. The Wormshill turn is signposted on the right. (If you get as far as the Bredgar and Wormshill Railway you have missed the turn.) Take the Wormshill turn and at the far end turn right. Blacksmiths Arms is on the left.
Sat Nav ME9 0TU.
Parking: There is on-street parking in the village or at Blacksmiths Arms.
OS Map: Explorer 148 Maidstone & the Medway Towns.
Grid ref: TQ878570.

Terrain: A few hundred metres of road walking with more on the alternative route avoiding some quite challenging terrain and stiles. The terrain is undulating with a series of small but sometimes steep valleys to negotiate. Footpaths and tracks can get muddy in winter.
Livestock: Sheep can be encountered at various places.
Stiles: None on the easier route but if you choose the alternative route beyond point 4 there is a series which have been wired up.
Nearest vets: Harrietsham Vets, Unit 9, Roebuck Business Park, Ashford Rd, Harrietsham, Maidstone, ME17 1AB. ☎ 01622 858666.

THE PUB **BLACKSMITHS ARMS** is an independently owned free house in the centre of the village, but it is not always open during the day. ☎ 01622 884386 to check.

As an alternative try the atmospheric and intriguingly named **DIRTY HABIT** in Harrietsham, just down the road. You will have driven past it on your

right-hand side as you started to climb the hill through Harrietsham on your way to Wormshill from the A20. Recently restored, it retains its period charm and character including a Georgian oak bar and Victorian furniture. Set on the Pilgrims' Way, the site of the pub dates from the 11th century when monks brewed and sold ale to pilgrims on their way to Canterbury.
⊕ elitepubs.com/the-dirty-habit
☎ 01622 880880

The Walk

1 With your back to Blacksmiths Arms turn left. Walk down the lane and take the first footpath a few metres further on the right-hand side. Follow the path across the field. Follow the path as it dips down into a gentle valley and into some trees at the other side. Go through the gate at the top and follow the path as it

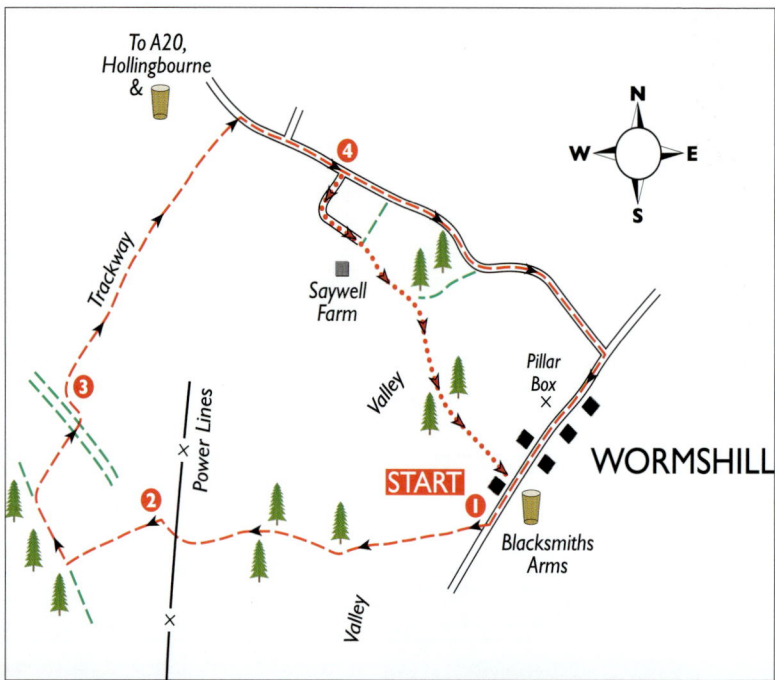

crosses the next field at an approximate 30° angle from the right-hand tree line. At the other end of the field the path broadens and drops down through some trees. At the bottom bear left along the valley. The path then climbs to the right passing underneath the power lines to the top of the hill.

❷ Go through the gate at the top. You now need to keep next to the left-hand field line for a short distance then cross the stile on the left in the fence line. At the time of our visit this had been covered in wire but there was a gate a few feet further on. You now go straight across the next field. When you reach the woods on the far side turn right following the track.

❸ Where the track emerges onto a lane cross straight over. You now follow the same track as it twists and turns through the woods. Where it emerges onto a lane, turn right. Walk up the road until the roads diverge.

❹ Here you have a choice. If you and your dog can cope with challenging terrain and stiles with no dog passages plus some steep and narrow paths through dense shrubbery, bear right here. If not, bear left and keep following the road to the very end. At the end turn right noting the Victorian pillar box on the right-hand side. Continuing along the lane past the houses you will be back at Blacksmiths Arms.

For the more adventurous beware, this is a difficult route. Bear right at point 4, follow the lane as it turns left and continue ahead until the lane bears right and there is a footpath sign on the left. At this point keep straight ahead and follow the path as it crosses two stiles. Where it emerges from the scrub continue across the next field. In the next set of woods it will drop steeply down into a valley. Follow it to the far right-hand corner of the field at the valley bottom. Walk up through the woods and when you emerge at the top follow the path straight ahead at the next field. At the far side you will pass between some gardens and come out onto the lane almost opposite the pub.

A SELECTION OF OTHER DOG FRIENDLY COUNTRY PUBS IN KENT

COBHAM – Darnley Arms.
COLDRED – The Carpenters Arms.
CRANBROOK – White Horse.
COWDEN – The Fountain Inn.
DUNGENESS – The Britannia.
EAST FARLEIGH – The Bull
EASTRY – The Five Bells.
EYNSFORD – The Five Bells, The Plough Inn.
FRITTENDEN – The Bell & Jorrocks.
GODDEN GREEN – The Bucks Head.
GRAVENEY – The Freewheel.
GREEN STREET GREEN – The Queens Head, The Royal Oak.
GROOMBRIDGE – The Crown, The Junction.
HALSTEAD – The Rose & Crown.
HORTON KIRBY – The Bull.
HERNE – The Butchers Arms.
HILDENBOROUGH – The Plough Inn.
IGHTHAM COMMON – Old House.
KEMSING – The Bell.
LAMBERHURST – Elephants Head.
LEEDS – The Park Gate Inn.
LOWER HALSTOW – The Three Tuns.
LUDDESDOWN – The Cock Inn.
OARE – Three Mariners, The Castle.
RECULVER – The King Ethelbert Inn.
PENSHURST – The Leicester Arms Hotel, The Bottle House.
RUSTHALL – Toad Rock Retreat.
RYARSH – Duke of Wellington.
SEVENOAKS WEALD – The Windmill.
SNARGATE – The Red Lion.
STANSTED – The Black Horse.
TEMPLE EWELL – The Fox Inn.
UPNOR – The Kings Arms.

APPLEDORE – The Ferry Inn.
BARFRESTONE – The Wrong Turn.
BENENDEN – The Bull.
BETHERSDEN – The George.
BISHOPSBOURNE – The Mermaid.
BRAMLING – The Haywain.
BRENCHLEY – Halfway House.
BROADSTAIRS – Thirty Nine Steps Brewhouse.
CHARING – The Bowl Inn.
CHILHAM – The White Horse.
CHELSFIELD – The Five Bells.
CHIDDINGSTONE CAUSEWAY – The Little Brown Jug.